My Next Husband Will Be A Lesbian

A COLLECTION OF STORIES FROM
WOMXN FINDING THEIR TRUTH

Stories Written & Collected by
Pasha Marlowe

GWN Publishing

GhostWritersNetwork.com

My Next Husband Will Be A Lesbian
A Collection Of Stories From Womxn Finding Their Truth

GhostWriters Network Publishing
GhostWritersNetwork.com
A Division of LongBar Creative Solutions, Inc. (LBCS)
LongBarCreatives.com

Edited by: Lil Barcaski, Katelyn Stewart, and Linda Hinkle
Cover Design: Cyndi Long - LBCS/GFADDesign *GFADDesign.com*

Book Layout ©2021 GFADDesign.com

My Next Husband Will Be A Lesbian / Pasha Marlowe. —1st ed.
ISBN 978-1-7336929-9-1

Dedication

In loving memory of my previous self who, just before disappearing, realized the one thing she had not yet tried... being seen.

Contents

What Others Are Saying

Stories are the lifeblood of human experience. It takes courage to invite other humans into your story, and that is exactly what these womxn did for the benefit of us all. Human sexuality and relationships are complex, and it serves us to open our hearts and minds to that complexity. Truth telling about sex and relationships is a revolutionary act. "My Next Husband Will Be a Lesbian" is just that—a revolution in what is possible when we honor our deepest authenticity.

Relationships, sex, and sexuality are complex and made even more complex by the negative sex culture many of us endure around the world. Living as a person whose sexuality doesn't adhere to what culture deems as acceptable or "normal" is a constant source of dissonance for those who are gay, lesbian, queer, trans, nonbinary, asexual, bisexual, pansexual, and beyond. If you are a womxn or a person of color, the impact of the intersectionality creates even more need to wear your armor.

And yet, armor is heavy and wearing it all the time is challenging. That level of self-protection can wear you down. That's why community among those of us who live and love beyond the norm is imperative to our health and wellness. When we witness each other, we are looking in a mirror that brings peace and ease, rather than fraught self-examination. The stories we share with one another are balm, and the mutual support is sustenance to keep us vibed up.

For these womyn to invite you into their stories is a revolutionary act. As a sexologist, I work with humans of every stripe to find their path to live and love in bliss and peace. I have been invited into the suffering, the struggles, the self-reflection fueled by seeking acceptance, so I know that when these powerful humans put pen to paper or hands to keyboard that act was not taken lightly. It is an act of revolution, an act of revolution in self-acceptance, in defiance of hate, and in support of the vast diversity in human sexuality. I invite you to commune with these stories with an open mind, open heart, and perhaps most importantly with respect for the vulnerability these authors have shared. Every human is their own universe. There is such exquisite beauty in honoring human complexity. May we all revel in and be enriched by these stories shared in love.

~ Krista A. H. Haapala
Sexologist and Consciousness Guide

Pasha Marlowe, standing in her light and truth, makes me want to scream from the rooftops! As an OB/GYN, I have the honor of holding space and hearing womxn's most sacred dreams, fears, and truths. This book is holding space for all womxn to know that their story is accepted and honored.

You are safe.

~ Dr. Lisa Parsons, D.O.

The compilation book, My Next Husband Will be a Lesbian, is a work of human art created for and by womxn who know the experience of a more expansive sexuality and relational reality but who have felt constrained and repressed in our culture to be who they have longed to be.

This book is a liberational act of self-love and courage gifted to its readers. It is my hope that those who are fortunate enough to read this book will find an accepting home here and may these authors' words to be one further step toward an inclusive, expansive world community where we accept our sexual nature, experience its healing power, and freely express it. Praise to Pasha Marlowe for creating this communal space and all the brave womxn who are the heroines of their stories.

~ *Jennifer Wiessner*
Healthy Sexuality, LCSW, AASECT Certified Sex Therapist

Pasha: The Messy Middle

The title "My Next Husband Will Be a Lesbian" came to me, like a calling, over a decade ago. I knew in my bones that I needed to write it, but I figured it would be a comedic piece about my frustration with men, the patriarchy ... and penises in general. I mean, doesn't every woman dream of running away to a women's commune to spend their days in emotional sharing circles and their nights dancing braless around a fire? Doesn't skinny dipping sound more fun with humans who empathize with cellulite, c-section scars and loose labia?

Over the past 10 years, however, more serious questions about my sexuality have risen, and the nature of this book changed. I began to ask questions, like:

Does every heterosexual woman have to imagine another woman to have an orgasm, as I do?

No?

So, does that make me a lesbian married to a man?

What if I have enjoyed some sex with men when I wasn't distracted by past sexual abuse, infidelities, and to-do lists?

Does that mean I am bi?

Do I have to have actual live experiences to back up these claims or can I identify as LGBTQ+ if all the knowing is in my head?

Netflix says I am definitely on the spectrum.

I have been an LGBTQ+ advocate since high school and always curious about intimacy with women, but I am faithful to my husband, and a mom, for goodness sake! So, discerning if I am gay or bi or ... queer ... (is that word really okay now?) or any of the other letters in the alphabet soup has been intimidating. I am still trying to learn all the terms and pronouns. There sure is a lot of grammatical confusion in inclusion!

Besides, my second husband and I finally figured out how to live together after 14 years of marriage. He does the dishes, I cook. He takes out the trash, I control the thermostat. He has affairs, I work on forgiveness. Why would I give this up? Oh, and we are saving for retirement, so when we turn 80, we can take up a hobby, like traveling in an RV and visiting imaginary grandchildren. We are even talking about moving to the suburbs soon, so our son can ride his bike to school, and we can eat s'mores at neighborhood BBQs.

If I were to decide to come out, what would that even look like? Coming out is for people who are not so ... rooted, right? Also, would I even be accepted in the LGBTQ+ world? Sure, I lead queer support groups and wear "Love is Love" shirts, and I may have ordered rainbow hair attachments, but I am a menopausal woman. It's like an awkward second adolescence, this time with chin hair and a dry vulva. Who knows if a woman will want to have sex with me or if my parts will even work? Plus, I am stuck in my ways and too tired to learn new tricks.

So, why write this from the messy middle of figuring out what I want and who I am? Wouldn't it make sense to wait and see how my romantic life unfolds BEFORE writing the damn book? Maybe. Wouldn't it be more logical to come out to my friends before disclosing it in a book? Well, sure. I'll do a group zoom reveal. Even if I were to write this here very book about my sexuality, it should be when my children are adults and my parents and my dreams are already dead, right? It wouldn't feel right to make waves right now, given the state of the world. Life is challenging enough for everyone.

I certainly wouldn't write a book during a pandemic when book tours and live speaking engagements are all but impossible. Not to mention that coming out as queer during a national lockdown is the worst timing ever. Even if I did actually want to start socializing in the LGBTQ+ community, meeting new people in person could literally kill me. Also, while my husband is fully aware that I am writing this book, he doesn't actually think I am going to publish it ... or suggest people read it!

Honestly, if this book already existed, without me and my friends having to write it, that would be great! I would have LOVED to have a "Maybe Bi-Bible" or "Poly for the Pollyannish" or "I Want an Abby!" to reference while figuring out my plan. There are a few books out there about navigating sexuality in heteronormative marriages, but they don't represent Generation X-Z and none come in large font, which just seems cruel. I wanted a book that felt like I was holding up a mirror to my soul. I wanted to know my options!

So here we are.

I am monogamous and traditional and really quite boring.

I am in bed before 10 p.m. and am shy at parties.

I have long hair, styled equally on both sides, no tattoos, and I eat meat.

I've been playing the game of life for 50 years and have always shoved a blue peg beside me in the tiny plastic car. Is there a bench seat option for a pink peg to hang with us up front?

Only in trucks, you say? Go figure.

I owned a minivan and I liked it. The more kids in there, the better. There, I said it.

And isn't the polyamorous lifestyle for people who are promiscuous and believe in unicorns?

Would that arrangement make me the bottom of the "V"? And if she's married, are we a "W"?

Honestly, some days I don't have enough time for a shower, much less a second partner.

I can't imagine how any of this seems like a good idea.

I am better off just leading support groups and encouraging others to speak their radical truths out loud and on comedy stages.

My good enough life is fine for me, though I would never encourage another woman to settle for a "good enough" or "fine" life for herself, so that's odd.

I am my own worst client sometimes.

What if everything changes in my life after I publish this book?

Or, even worse, what if NOTHING changes?

Did I mention I haven't slept well in decades?

Every time I go to my doctor, she tells me my hormones are out of balance, my cortisol levels are through the roof, and I need to "calm the fuck down."

She gave me a medical marijuana card, but I am too nervous to use it.

I am one of those people who doesn't do drugs, drink, or even jaywalk.

I am probably just a straight woman with ADHD and an aversion to routine.

Only, I have tried all the righteous or "woke" things to feel better. Therapy, yoga, acupuncture, earthing, journaling, celery juice, sticky note affirmations, finding work that lights me up, finding vibrators that light me up, chocolate dipped in peanut butter, and I still do not feel well.

Anxiety, chronic pain, and fantasies of scissoring plague me.

I think holding my thoughts inside my brain is killing me.

Can you relate?

Do you have secrets stuck inside your body that cause you pain?

My throat is sore, my chest is heavy, and my hips have been replaced.

If I wasn't menopausal, I would think I was pregnant. My pelvis is swollen and leaky.

It's like another person is growing inside of me, but I am too rusty and afraid to birth her.

What will happen if she is revealed to the world?

What if all of these longings are better off simply left unsaid?

What if I never experience being with a woman, and I feel my life was unlived?

What if I finally have the experience and I don't even like it?

What if I realize that sex never feels safe or fun?

What if I find her and then she leaves me?

What if my husband decides this isn't a good idea?

What if I walk directly into the fire and burn?

What if I walk out of the fire and rise?

What if my home is built from those ashes?

What if I actually stand in my power without fear of judgement?

What if I stop playing small and practice what I preach?

What if I speak my mind, even though my voice is shaking*?

What if just one story in this book liberates one woman to stand proudly in her truth?

What if just one prompt from the end of this book sparks an honest conversation in a marriage that leads to hope and creative solutions?

What if just one word from these brave women brings awareness and compassion to one parent of a child questioning their sexuality?

What if this book can reduce shame and loneliness and save a life?

Now I remember the calling to reveal all of the heartache and hilarity. The title is messy because the mess is the message. It isn't easy, it's just true, and the possibilities are plentiful.

*Maggie Kuhn said, "Speak your mind even if your voice shakes."

Well, The Problem Is You Have a Dick

Sex. I like it. I guess. Kinda.

Okay, in truth, I like the IDEA of it enough to keep attempting the recreation of what I always thought it should be. After years of exposure to heteronormative interpretations in movies, books, Cosmo's "10 Ways to Keep Him Interested" articles, music, art, ads, TV shows (okay, ALL the media), you can imagine me surprised, after 27 years of marriage, to find myself still at a loss identifying the problem that kept me from feeling what I saw represented in all these mediums my entire life. Obviously, something was wrong with me. I easily created excuses as to why the mystery of intimacy and sexual enjoyment still eluded me. Past trauma, check. Parenting and kids, check. Busy professional careers, check. Perimenopause, check. I had my list of reasons ready to act as a veritable shield when my brain tried to question whether or not it was natural to have never felt sexually or emotionally fulfilled.

My husband and I married at 20. He was safe, he was kind, and he met the image of what I was supposed to want and desire. I was not about to let that comfort and growing love get away from me when it so beautifully framed what I had been taught was the ultimate goal: find a man, settle down, have babies, grow old together. For the most part, that's what happened. The thing is men were never the only sex I found attractive. The first time I can remember getting butterflies in my stomach (Thank you, Debbie Harry) I found it wasn't the "boy" that was catching my eye. I never did look too deeply at this part of myself; I knew if I did, I would have to spend time analyzing and accepting some truths that, quite frankly, didn't fit into the pretty little box of normalcy I was creating about myself. At this point, I figured our lack of sexual experience and exploration was the cause of the awkward, fumbling, mess that became the standard for our sex life for the next 27 years. There were times I dreaded sex. The hair on my arms would raise like I was being stalked by a serial killer (and it felt like it, too) when I heard the words, "Hey, wanna do it?" Often, I did, just to get it over with. Just as often, we would go six to eight months never having once done the deed. I resigned myself to the fact that this is just what sex really was in a marriage, and I took comfort in the fact that at least I could count on my husband to always be one of my best friends, my continued safe space.

But life is funny isn't it? I thought that just because I was holding the paddles I was in control of the boat. I thought if I just accepted things as they were, I could continue gliding down calm waters until I reached the end of my journey. That's when I hit the rapids. I read "Untamed" by Glennon Doyle. My world was turned upside down. Here, written as if directly to me, were all the things I was scared to look at too closely as my life progressed down the charted, navigated journey I had created to make a safe and secure space in which to survive. I felt confused, angry, and an unwavering dedication to stop being scared of what was to come and to embrace what could be. It was transformative. It was scary. But in the end, I unwaveringly found my truth.

When Covid hit, I decided to finally put on my big girl panties and start seeing a therapist. Yes, I am the definition of procrastination. I was nervous about so many things. My calm waters were getting choppy and I knew I needed a river guide, or I was going under. I didn't want to be vulnerable. I wanted to be a Bad Ass Cheetah who didn't need anyone else to stay strong. Was she going to make me drudge up the events of my past? Could I handle reliving those thoughts and emotions while stuck in a house, isolated with only my husband as a companion? The lack of intimacy had grown over the years and had grown into a lack of communication and ultimately, anger. I wasn't sure I was ready to handle the rough waters I was headed toward without an outlet for emotions I had buried for so long. But there, in that strange world of digital rooms, I found safety. And I finally said what I had been afraid to say all along, "I am a lesbian."

I was right, however. It was too hard to live with someone who I didn't feel ready to share myself with. My therapist equates this time of confinement to a "pressure cooker" waiting to blow. Because I had reached maximum pressure, I felt it was too hard to have a rational and emotional conversation. I simply no longer felt emotionally safe with my husband the way I had tried to force myself to believe I was. I just couldn't do it. I was stuck in this limbo. So, I did what most rational and sane people should do when faced with a life-altering crisis. I turned to social media. I started searching anywhere and everywhere to see if there were others like me. People who deep down knew something was up but had let time and life slip by because it was all good enough. Who were looking back at it all and wondering WTF was I thinking by waiting so long? What have I missed? Hell, my boobs are trying to help me out by becoming floatation devices to help with my turbulent waters. How will this not make it so I spend this next part of my journey alone? Crazy thing is, I found that apparently there are A LOT of women who are asking these same questions. I wasn't alone. I met amazing women who shared their stories with me, who were facing many of the same issues, and I finally had this space to build my strength and to start doing the hard things. And I did.

The 100th "Hey baby, wanna do it?" came and I simply could not find another excuse, another way to say no, I just couldn't find a way to avoid my answer yet again. I took a deep breath and said, "You know when you keep asking me about having sex, I feel guilty saying no all the time." My husband just looked at me and then asked if that meant that I should be the one to initiate it and he should wait ... or was it something else? HERE, at this moment, my brain decided to inform me that, "This is yet another chance to come right out and tell him," was being placed right into your lap, so, whatcha gonna do, sister friend? So, I took a breath and very tactfully replied, "Well, the problem is you have a dick" because I am slick like that. While he had a "What?" moment, I took a deep breath and told him everything. I told him that I no longer wanted to have sex with men. At all!

But you know what?

He has been amazing. He has had his moments of "are there things I could have done?" and "want to just get a girlfriend together?" But he answers himself before I even have to utter the words. He told me he is proud of me. I told him my biggest fear out of all of this was that I would lose him as my person, my best friend. He said that would never happen because I am his person and his best friend. It is not all fixed... there are good hours and bad hours for me and for him, but he has also said a lot of things about how he knew he had a responsibility for our relationship too. He also said that he procrastinated getting a couple's therapist right before quarantine because he had a feeling it was going to be the bridge that led to us separating. I love that he shared that. Things are progressing at warp speed.

I told all the kids. They are all adults, so this is a lot easier for me to do now. I told my boss (since my husband and I work in the same department). She was so amazing that when I brought it up and assured her that of course nothing would change because my husband and I are still best friends, she said that the thought didn't even cross her mind. She just wants us to be okay. I can never leave this job now.

He told his sister, his dad, and his best friend, his super lesbian best friend. (I was a bit nervous about that, but she sent me a text to say she loves me, and she is here for me).

He is trying to look at houses, he is trying to figure out how to sell things and enter into a new world of dating and making friends. He is un-nesting on hyper mode. He is packing.

So, I made it through the first set of rapids without drowning in the turbulent waters. I have support. I have a best friend in my husband that will not break just because our lives will look differently than I had charted for the both of us. Mostly though, I am settled and peaceful in a way I have never experienced in my lifetime and just, maybe, I am excited about embracing the churning and swelling waters ahead.

~ Shannon Gregory

Katelyn's Story

I grew up the byproduct of a tumultuous marriage and an even more volatile divorce. Neither of my parents liked each other and they spent nine years fighting over custody of me. Eventually, both of my parents would remarry other people, unsuccessfully, I might add, and in my young, child-like brain, I became desensitized to failing marriages and false promises of love. But I would hear my father talk longingly of beautiful women and my mother talk fondly of handsome men and somewhere along the way, I knew I felt the same way as both of my parents; I was fond of handsome women.

My mother grew up a very strict Catholic, but we became Baptists when she married my ex-stepfather. Nonetheless, in both branches of Christianity, it was certain that romantic love is only meant for a man and woman. Homosexual relationships were not even recognized as real relationships, just sinful acts inspired by the Devil to make God vomit. Lucky for me, it was only the homosexual men that had to look out for God's condemning hand and as I was well on my way to becoming a woman, I would have nothing to worry about if I thought about kissing another woman. That was until someone in the church made it clear that lesbians were just as detestable as gay men.

As a good Christian girl should, I began searching for the man of my dreams. Unfortunately, "he" with the long, dark hair and slender frame always became "she" with the long, dark hair and slender frame, when things became quiet. I spent years trying to alter my thoughts as I was once again informed that God knew everything I was thinking.

God became a second father, and I was always embarrassed when the thoughts would pass through me. Finally, when I was 11, my prayers paid off, and I stopped fantasizing about women. Finally, I was ready to embrace the manliest man that God had put on this Earth for little ol' straight me.

And so, it began. I was homeschooled until my 8th-grade year, and the summer before, I met a boy at church camp who fit the previously desirable description: dark hair, almond eyes, and thin wrists that I found enchanting. We skipped youth meetings to go kiss under the stairs, and I knew that he was the one. Until he realized that I wasn't, and he held hands with one of my friends. I felt terribly confused by this because a) He was the man of my godly dreams and b) The girl he liked was nothing like the girls that used to be in mine (he was blonde and plump). I became unbelievably insecure and began searching for any thin, dark-haired boy I could find to finally redeem the situation.

My transition to 8th grade public school was fantastic, except for the normal rumors that are spread about new girls who were previously homeschooled. My favorite was the one where they said I had put a cat in the microwave. My least favorite was the one where they said I was a lesbian. "How dare they!"

I thought. "I have put way too much energy into NOT being a lesbian for these cocksuckers to say that I am!"

Aside from being severely disliked, fate would smile on me as a new friend would come to my aid. She took me under her heterosexual wing and taught me all I needed to know about boys and what to do with them. Everything was going great until she came over to my house one night.

My hopes that this hard-hitting heterosexual female was there to teach me the ways of womanly wiles were trashed as we became each other's first girl kiss.

We never talked again.

High school began to pass smoothly, with no more interruptions from late-night female encounters, but the boys I dated were always boring, and even though I smiled at them, I never felt much.

When I was 16, I was driving with my dad to visit my family out West. Every time we would see a girl running, he would lose it over their outward beauty. I couldn't but help notice how right he was. As my father is a strict agnostic and had no problem with people being gay or not, I decided that I would tell him that I may find women beautiful like he did. For a moment there was silence, and then he started laughing hysterically, saying very loudly, "Oh, yeah! You like licking that pussy, do you?!"

I never talked about it with him again. Years went by and boys came and went. Always slender with long dark hair.

When finally, it happened. I had gotten a part in a touring musical theater production and friends from work were throwing me a going away party. A long-haired, thin hippie came up to me and started talking my ear off. His personality was just as bizarre as mine, and I found him extremely funny. He asked me if I'd like to go out with him sometime, and when I told him that I was leaving in the morning, he pulled a tiger's eye ring off his finger that his father had given him and gave it to me.

After my run in the musical was up, I came back home feeling lost and defeated. One evening, I decided to write the long-haired hippie, asking if he would like to join me for a cigarette.

He picked me up in his brother's car, slightly drunk, and much to my surprise, with a shaven head, and we drove around for about an hour listening to Talking Heads and smoking cigarettes. Afterward, he dropped me off at my house and left.

Over the next few weeks, we would meet up to smoke cigarettes and go on walks, delving into each other's pasts. One night, with the aid of much alcohol, I told him, "I might be bi." And he said, "I might be too." That's when we decided to elope with the thought that, "Two wrongs make a right." We were married on a hill with only his brother and my sister as witnesses. As we were driving away from the hill, "You're My Best Friend" by Queen came on the radio and I remember thinking how happy I was going to be with the man that I also felt was my best friend.

But nothing was ever all right. As time passed, it became quite clear that we were both far less "Bi" than we had discussed. He began to drink more, and I became a chimney. He would disappear with friends for days at a time and call me crying in the middle of the night to come to find him. One night, I found him in a parking lot, completely drunk, and he told me something that had happened to him as a child at the hands of a babysitter. We both cried together, and I brought him home.

Then it was my turn to breakdown. He was building a room in the garage and I had been acting like a villain since before I could remember. I finally broke down and cried, knowing that I wasn't being honest with myself. I went out to the garage and sat on a ladder. He looked at me and asked what was wrong. I told him, "I think I'm gay." He stopped what he was doing, laid the drill down, pulled out a cigarette, and lit it. He walked over to me and handed it to me. I looked at him with tears in my eyes and asked, "What are we going to do?"

He never answered. I decided that I had to file for divorce.

As far as divorces go, ours was easy. We fought a little over our dog, but I would call him to check and make sure he was doing all right. As time went on, he responded less and less until one day, three weeks after our papers were finalized, he called me.

It was midnight, and as I answered half asleep, I heard him say, "I thought you might like it if I came over for some closure." Sleepily, I told him that would be fine.

We sat outside my house talking and smoking cigarettes like we used to. I will never forget the things that were said that night, and I made him a very serious promise not to repeat certain things under the condition he never hurt himself.

Two nights later, he started a high-speed chase in a city, ran his car into a grassy lot, fired shots in the air, and was gunned down by the two police officers chasing him.

There are days when I look at openly gay men and think to myself, "He might have been so happy with them."

I only hope in his next life, his wife will be a better husband.

As for me, my next husband will be my first wife.

~ Katelyn

Spatula Moments

I like you," she said to me.

"I like you too!" I said back to her.

"No, you don't understand, I REALLY like you," she said.

"I REALLY like you too," I said back again.

"No, I don't think you are getting it. I like you a lot ... I "like-like" you – not just as a friend. I want to touch you and kiss you and do other things with you."

"Oh," I said back to her in a way that wasn't shocked or surprised but intrigued. With only a slight pause I said, "I think that I would like that too."

Fast forward a couple of weeks and I am kissing her, and my new favorite thing is feeling and watching her orgasm. It's different. I feel different. I love it.

During this time, I was completely in the moment, and I didn't dwell for one second how my physical and emotional intimacy with her may possibly define my sexuality. I just knew that I liked it. My brain didn't allow me to register it on any level other than that it was an event that happened in my life. As if I had just taken a lovely trip to the county fair, and now it's over and I'm onto the next thing. I still don't understand why my brain chose to ignore this important piece of information about myself, and later I will spend years beating myself up about "not figuring this out sooner" when I finally admit my truth to myself.

Societal and familial heteronormative expectations that were engrained in me likely played a role in the suppression of my sexuality, however I don't want to dwell on this part of my story because there are experts that have written and explained these topics masterfully. I do, however, remember a specific moment when my dad expressed being nervous about me choosing to go to a women's college because it might "turn me into a lesbian." I was 17 years old, and my mother and I laughed the comment off, but the message was clear—a daughter that is a lesbian is disappointing, something to be feared (hence the nervousness) and not valued within the family. As a people pleasing do-gooder, this did not fit who I wanted to be. I did not want to be a disappointment. I did not want to be different. I did not want to be talked about and judged. The truth is I wanted to be accepted and I wanted a "normal" life. I wanted a husband, a house, and kids. Also, I wasn't repulsed by men, so I was able to be with them which made things even more confusing. In the end, it doesn't matter how and why I missed or dismissed it. I think it is human nature to want answers, so I have just accepted that this is how my story unfolded.

I am now standing in my kitchen. I am 33 years old, with a beautiful 2 ½ year-old son, a husband that I love, and a life that makes me happy. I remember standing in my kitchen and saying quietly to myself, "I am gay." The words settled inside me, and it felt right. It was like I found a piece of a puzzle to myself that finally fits and makes sense. I felt warm, comforted, and happy in that moment, however, in the very next moment, a different and longer lasting feeling of terror set in and created a fear that lasted for the next 11 ½ years. The fear comes from knowing I have this life that I built that doesn't match my insides, and that the only way to correct it will cause hurt, loss, grief, and financial insecurity. I realize quickly that change or no change will result in tremendous loss. Loss of either my traditional family unit, my best friend, and feelings of security and safety, or the loss of my true self. All these losses are unbearable, and I felt a deep sense of hopelessness as I worked to sort through my feelings.

I found a therapist and I scoured the internet for answers (which is never where you never find answers to questions like these). The internet did, however, help me find an online support group, that was extremely helpful. It was the first time that I found others that had later-in-life realizations that they had an attraction to women and found themselves in heterosexual marriages. I finally felt less alone. Unfortunately, my husband found my internet searches and confronted me about my sexuality before I was ready to have that conversation. I told him where I was at with my feelings, and there was a lot of uncertainty, anxiety, and tears. I had no answers for him because I wasn't ready for the conversation, and it felt traumatic. After the initial trauma, however, I did feel freer having him know and being able to have conversations around my sexuality.

The woman who ran the online support group also ran a retreat/workshop in Philadelphia for married women who are questioning their sexuality. My husband encouraged me to attend because he was anxious for answers and needed clarity as much as I did. I went to the retreat and met amazing women that were struggling with many of the same questions, anxieties, and guilt as me. Feeling seen and not alone was extremely helpful. I came home and spent the next several months figuring out with my husband what our next steps should be. The truth was that I was happy with my life, and I absolutely knew that I did not want to miss out on significant time with my son while he was little. I decided that I wanted to stay. I was not in a miserable marriage, and I would just have to figure out how to manage my feelings around my sexuality. I decided that sexuality is only just a part of me and that I could surely manage this part of myself. I would just be a lesbian that is married to a man. Easy enough, right? I spent most of the next 10 years distracting myself with family, friends, and work. Periodically, my sexuality and feelings of not being where I am supposed to be would pop up, but I was able to acknowledge those feelings and move on.

Over the past couple of years, I began to struggle more with feelings of inauthenticity and eventually, hiding who I am to my family and my friends became intolerable. I agreed to hide my sexuality with a few exceptions because my husband wasn't comfortable with me being out while we were married. At the time, it seemed like this was a reasonable to way to honor him, and because I felt so guilty for not figuring myself out before we got married. I built a flimsy dam inside me to hold back the truth, but over time, the pressure created inevitable cracks that became too much, and I eventually ran out of fingers and toes to stop the leaks. I was nonchalantly dropping hints to people about women I found attractive. I started dressing the way that felt more natural to me, and I bought clothes with rainbows any chance I could get. It was all leaking out of me, and I was trying to scream my truth without actually saying a word. It felt like my inner self was refusing to be denied no matter how hard I tried to push back or how inconvenient it was to my life. I could feel myself reaching a breaking point.

The problem is that being gay is bigger than just having sex with the right person. This truth and feeling of loss were growing inside me and infecting many of my waking thoughts. I was reading a lot of Brené Brown at the time and listening to many of her interviews. I was starting to lean into her concepts of vulnerability, courage, shame, being clear, having difficult conversations, and being brave enough to stand alone. It was from this reading that I decided I needed to have another conversation with my husband. It was 10 years after I recommitted to our marriage. I was terrified. I was so terrified that I decided that we needed a new word to describe the specific fear you feel in that nanosecond just before revealing yourself and leaping into the unknown without knowing what lies on the other side. I suppose the word for that is "vulnerability," but in that moment, I just really wanted a new word. I told my husband that I needed to be out to more of my family and friends. I told him that part of me was dying because I was hiding such a big part of myself, and I could not take it anymore. I truly believe that concealment of your truth has significant consequences over time. I wasn't looking to end my marriage or even be with a woman when I spoke to him. What I needed was to be able to be fully authentic with all of the people in my life. He thanked me for being honest and for talking to him and then asked if he could think about it and get back to me later.

Ten months later, he got back to me and asked me for a divorce. There was no anger. He was extremely supportive, and he did not want me to feel guilty at all. He took all of that time to plan almost every step of our split. It almost feels ridiculous that I had no idea. We've had this conversation a few times before, but it was different this time for both of us. It was the first time I didn't stop him or beg for this not to happen. I was in shock, but I also knew deep down that it was right. I was both devastated and relieved. Over the past few months, I've come out to all of my friends, family, and co-workers, filed a separation agreement with the court, helped my husband pick out new curtains for his apartment, and watched my son's heart break in half when we told him about our impending divorce.

There have been so many hard moments, but I find that some of the hardest moments lie in the smallest of things. As an example, our spatula broke a couple of months ago. Typically, a spatula breaking is not a sad event, but when I went to Amazon to order a new one, my husband said, "you should probably order two." His comment stopped me. It quickly became one of the saddest purchases I have ever made and threw into focus how difficult the next few months were going to be. Since then, I have had many "spatula moments" as I now call them. So many that I would like to officially coin the saying "spatula moment." A "spatula moment" is when a seemingly small thing hits you like a ton of bricks, and for a moment, brings into focus the enormity of the emotional change that is or has occurred. The most recent "spatula moment" for me came in the grocery store when I realized that my husband had enough cereal to get him through the next week and that I will never buy him another box of cereal again. I wish my brain could pass over these moments, but I feel like I am a finely tuned machine that is designed to recognize anything remotely emotional or sentimental.

Since my husband and I are incredibly amicable, we are helping each other in any way we can. I recently saw his new apartment which is only a half-mile from our house, and I helped him move a washer, dryer, and the heaviest motherfucking king-sized bed into his apartment. My son gave me a tour of the apartment, which was awesome and weird. He hugged me twice while we were there, and I don't know if it was for him or for me. At one point when he was showing me around, we heard my husband coming up the stairs, and my son wanted to hide on him. We were standing in what is to be my husband's new bedroom, and my son pulls me into his closet to hide. So, I was standing there and realizing that I am literally hiding in my soon-to-be ex-husband's bedroom closet. The comedic irony was not lost on me and was seriously ridiculous.

Our change and his move happen to coincide with the holidays. Our last unaltered day as a family before he starts moving will be Christmas Day, and our last night together will be New Year's Eve. A crystal ball will literally drop at midnight to signify the end of our 20-year relationship and the disastrous year of 2020. Did I mention that I'm a frontline healthcare worker working with patients with Covid-19 all day long? It all feels very dramatic. Like if I were writing this as a fictional story in a book, the editor would probably tell me that I need to tone it down. I don't have hindsight yet to be able to look back at this time and tell you that it all worked out for the best and that we are all okay, but I can tell you that I feel like it will all be okay eventually. I have recently done every hard thing that I have been afraid of for so long, and I can say that this feels like the right kind of hard. Being stuck, living inauthentically, and having those same intrusive thoughts swirling in my head was worse in a way that it is very hard to describe. I can finally deal with actual problems instead of the thousand imaginary ones that I created in my head. I can say that I am finally moving in a direction that feels true. I know that something beautiful is at the end because I can feel it, even though I have no idea what it is. I guess what I have is hope. My story will continue to unfold with life's ups and downs, but I can finally put to rest the chapter of my life that has been defined by inauthenticity and fear that plagued me for far too long. I can say for the first time in my life that I am here, and I can walk into any room as my full and complete self.

~ Amanda

Blood, Sweat, & Tears- Nope!
Blood, Booms, & Fears

I wanted to tell my "back story" to this "coming out" experience, but that would literally take a whole book. For this little chapter, the CliffNotes of getting me to my first lesbian encounter will have to suffice.

1. Bio Father was a child molester and cruel abuser. You do the math.

2. Super open family on BOTH sides, and many gay and bis in several generations going back if you listen carefully to the family "stories."

3. My only bio sibling is my sister, she is 18 months older and has been out since she was born. We ALL knew she was gay, and she was NEVER able to hide it. She came out of the womb a tomboy and grew into her gay self from there.

4. My mom divorced her 2nd husband (who raised us, and who I adore to this day) when I was 15 and married a bible thumper from Tennessee who would physically cringe if any of these three Northern women even said the word tampon out loud! Get the gist?!

5. Due to much of the above, I was my mother's only hope for a "normal" family. And for a long time, I took that duty very seriously.

So, skip forward. I spent 10 years doing what most survivors do while healing. I slept with anyone and any way I could trying to figure out WHAT THE HELL all these straight girls were so excited about! Not a single encounter with any penis was EVER enjoyable nor fulfilling in ANY way, and it certainly never felt good, let alone ... just WTH was all this about? I just didn't get it. Then, my sis and I ended up in college together. I started spending time with her and all her lesbian friends. I learned to love every bit of the life from the campfires and guitar nights, the Indigo Girls, and even the camaraderie and acceptance that only happens when a group of women are all on the same page and in the same space. It was so comfortable. Familiar. Relaxing. It was FREEING!!

I met a very butch gay woman while working a temp job. I was assigned to the Pillsbury Plant working as executive assistant to the foreman of Fluor Daniel Construction. We built the toaster strudel plant. I was also the tool check girl. Lori was an electrician and one night, while checking her tools in, she struck up a conversation about her needing an OB/GYN! Go figure. After weeks of bantering, and I guess flirting, she asked me to a movie.

I went!

I have ZERO memory of the movie. NONE, but ... when she walked me to my apartment door, it was absolutely pouring out. I let her come in to towel off, and we did a little shuffle dance as she tried to stay on the little 3' by 3' cheap linoleum entryway. As I closed the door, we ended up chest to chest, we were so close. I shut the door, turned around with my back to the door, feeling more than a little trapped and excited at the same time.

She kissed me. One lingering kiss.

One.

One kiss!

Omg!! I think I may have literally melted. The rest is a bit of a blur. I came to sitting in the little linoleum puddle of rainwater and felt tears of joy. I NEVER EVER had anyone kiss me and have it literally taken my breath away. Her lips lingered on mine, and they felt like velvet. There was still a bubble of heat surrounding me when my roomie found me there. I do not know how long I sat there and let it wash over me again and again. I wanted to relive that moment and memorize it. I was sure it was some fluke! I wanted to save it and NEVER ever lose that feeling.

The next day, she asked me if I wanted to watch the Fourth of July fireworks from the tiny construction dorm room she was sharing with her cousin, Mark (also gay). It was on the 7th floor or something.

I went.

I met her at her apartment complex. All the travelling workers were there in the parking lot partying. It was the first night off after a seven-day work week. We had some drinks, hung out for a while, and when it started to get near dusk, Lori said we should go grab the room in case Mark decided to bring his date there too. I stood at the threshold and took in the entire tiny room. To my left, there was enough room for two twin beds with a sheet hanging from the ceiling between them for some privacy. At the foot of the beds were a wall of cabinets and what was trying to be a makeshift kitchen. Directly in front of me was a small closet that served as a clothes closet and linen closet with a sheet for a curtain to cover it. Centered on the wall to the right was the door to a bathroom that had bright white '60s-style tiles from floor to ceiling and tiny white octagon tiles on the floor. It was all white; even all the crappy hotel towels were white. I was terrified. She maneuvered behind me, hung a Do Not Disturb sign on the outer doorknob and shut the door.

We went to the tiny window over the sink at the foot of the bed to watch the fireworks and she gave me another PGA Punch we had taken from the parking lot party. We sipped the drinks and watched the fireworks in total silence for what felt like days. I was on edge. I could feel the heat coming both of us. July in Central Tennessee with no AC unit was sweltering. And what was this weird tingling was that kept running from my toes to my fingers and settling in my stomach? Butterflies. Is that what those silly girls meant? I wondered what else I was "missing." She set her drink down, took mine and set it down. She pulled the clip from my hair and let it fall down the front of my white cotton eyelet tank top. She leaned in and kissed me. Velvet. Again. Tender. Knees shaking. Don't fall … don't miss this. More velvet.

Leaning on the counter, she pushed me back further and the fireworks in the tiny window lit up the tiny all-white room. We were on the small bed, then the other bed. The sheet between the beds fell. The closet sheet got hooked on something and it came down. All those white sheets and white beds and white cabinets with little white ruffled skirts tacked to the bottom of the counter came down too. The fireworks were going off and lighting the room with a flood of colored lights. Boom! All Green. BOOM! All Blue.

I laid next to her completely transformed and was not sure if I was drunk from the punch or if this was what those silly girls gossiped about. I was so hot laying there. We were sticking together from the love making and the heat of that hot July night. We were both soaked, the sheets were sticking to us and left us entwined in those white sheets.

It was so wet. It's was so humid.

I could feel the sweat all over me. She was lying next to me and I could hear her breathing. She lovingly rolled over and brushed hair from my eyes. Kissed me on the forehead, and then the lips. Velvet again. She whispered softly on my neck, "You ready to go join the party? Take the bathroom first. Take your time, feel free to shower if your hot, honey. Then we'll join the party for a while, so the crew won't spend the next week guessing what we were doing," she laughed. "MEN," she said and giggled like it was an inside joke I should know.

I do now. She handed me a wash rag and towel she had pulled from a small shelf over the bed. I took them and shakily walked to the bath while my knees were still so weak.

I reached my arm around the door frame, sliding my hand up and down one wall then the other looking for the light switch. I found it. I didn't want to spoil the mood by turning on the bright light in that white bath and spoil the magic of the fireworks still lighting up the skies. I noted the switch, left it off, and cracked the door to let in the firework lights.

MTSU, my college, was just a few blocks away. The stadium was lit up with fireworks, and it was about time for the finale. I slid against the counter till I was all the way in the bathroom. I shut my eyes and tried to replay what had just happened while my eyes adjusted to the dim light. I left the door cracked open while I tried to compose myself and not start giggling like an uncontrolled loon. I was in shock, I think. If it's possible to induce shock through multiple orgasms, then I was DEFINITELY in shock!

I was in my mid-20s. For the first time in my life, I knew what the silly girls were talking about. I was sure they had NO CLUE what a woman can do if they were so excited about those stupid boys! I felt like I had won the orgasm lottery! I stood and basked in the glow for several minutes till Lori's voice broke my trance. "Hey, I said shower, not do your laundry too!" she giggled "but seriously, I gotta pee, so you gotta hurry it up." I turned on the faucet and tried to wipe off with cool water. I was sticky. I was hot. It was so hot in there!

"Sorry, baby! It's your fault my knees won't work! I'll hurry." The fireworks started to slow down, and it was getting darker. I had to turn the light on to touch up my make-up and hair. I slowly slid the door closed and turned on the light.

I don't know how long I stood there. This time I KNOW I was in shock. I was frozen from fear, humiliation, panic, and embarrassment. I sat there in shock for what felt like hours. Like when you dream you have showed up to high school in your underwear. That complete and total debilitating fear of humiliation. I heard a light tapping on the door, "Baby, are you okay? Did I hurt you? Baby, say something. You're starting to worry me."

What could I say? How could I tell her that just before the door closed and after I had flipped that light switch, I saw the Texas Chainsaw Massacre! That all-white, tiny, little prison-cell-sized apartment? The walls, the sheets, the cabinets, and the floor were soaked through on both beds. I turned around in sheer terror with my back to the door, opened my eyes, and saw the white bathroom ... again, I saw that white tile bathroom. I had been leaning on the wall, sitting on the toilet lid in the dark, and then sitting on the edge of the rusting tub just moments before trying to wash my face in the dark. Everything I had touched, every spot I walked on had footprints, handprints, ass prints! I had slid my hand across every surface searching for the switch while trying to keep the magic light of the fireworks on as long as possible.

Blood! Period blood. Some of that stickiness was not just body fluids from all that sex. Some of that shit was ...

What do I do?

"Lori? I think we have a problem ... you may want to turn on the lights out there." I wanted the earth to swallow me right then.

"Jesus Christ!" she screamed.

Yup, every sheet, both beds and the floor were a bloody train wreck.

After surviving our first colorful encounter, Lori and I were together on and off for about four years. She taught me how to be gay, but more than that she showed me how to just be ME. How to stop hating my body for what was done to it and for what I had done to it while looking for ...

Her?

Answers?

The secret to life?

Or at least looking for the person that would give me the courage and permission to enjoy something about my sexuality. A couple years after we moved in together, Lori and I split up and I ended up quickly falling back into my old Great Straight Hope role. My mom never stopped reminding me of my "duty" to have her grandkids. Which btw, I have always known that I never wanted kids. So, who was I kidding?

After a long engagement and living with a new boyfriend, George, for several years in a mobile home while finishing my BS Degree, I left him, too, and met Paul. One horrible and destined-to-fail marriage later (and this did fail 6 months after we were married), I found what I thought I needed. Since then there have been a couple serious committed relationshps with women. All ending, but I have not givn up. Not sure if any of us ever finds that perfect partner/soulmate? No matter what sex they are or what gender anyone else identifies as. All we can do is hope and try and take chances.

The ONLY way to KNOW you found "the one" is if you can look at the person you are with and see yourself in a rocking chair on a porch, drinking lemonade in the future with both of you gray haired, overweight, and retired in each other's arms.

The only thing I am sure of is that other rocking chair will hold a woman.

~ Cyn

Natasha

Every so often, when my mind trembles on the cusp of a dream, my earthly body softens, like butter—all creamy and inviting—and I crave the lips of my almost-lover ... the one I lost so long ago.

She was ... the taste of delight. The honey of summer in a perfectly sun-ripened pear. The dew of morning. And the hush of Aspens as they whisper through cool mountain air ... "Na-taaaash-aaaahhh!"

Oh, Natasha!

Natasha. She is gone, and it is winter. I am a decade younger, but still, the wind howls through the trees. The world outside can only be seen in black and white, a thousand shades of gray.

Light from the fire is warm and soft, flooding my mind with memories of the summer sun. I can close my eyes and feel it on my skin, like a lover. Like Natasha. Long lost, returning for one last kiss.

And isn't it exquisite to crave the taste of summer on my tongue while surrounded by the fury of snow and ice? Far better than living in perpetual sunshine.

Just the thought of the sun's rays on the curve of my hip, the hollow of my throat, and the pulse of my wrist is enough to see me through the darkest days of winter.

Oh, Natasha.

Natasha.

Everything on Earth could remain draped in snow for a 100 years, that summer, a thing of the past. And yet, if I closed my eyes and called for it, gently, it would always return ... if only for me. For Natasha.

Oh, Natasha.

Natasha. You call to me without words, the heat emanating from your skin promising to warm the chill that has taken up permanent residence in my bones.

Here you are, the enticing gift that has haunted me throughout my existence, just waiting to be discovered again. Limbs quiver in anticipation as our bodies draw near.

Our first kiss ... it is a lifetime of rapture.

Encapsulated in One. Single. Unforgettable. Moment.

Oh, Natasha.

~ Dre

Carrie's Story

Even now, as a 47-year-old woman, I still cannot remember the sexual encounter that first began my experimentation and shaped my life. I remember playing doctor with two brothers and putting crayons between my labia with another girl. I remember finally saying no to my primary abuser, only to get in trouble with his mom after I spat on him for, what she thought, was because he was black. I remember getting caught with my hands down a boy's pants by my father, only to have my parents both "sit me down" and have a very vague talk about saying no if someone tells you to do something you don't want to do. Those were all before I was 12. In seventh grade, I gave my first voluntary blowjob. As I put his penis in my mouth, my immediate thought was, "This is the smell of a black man's penis." He was white. This experience not only triggered the recall of the sexual abuse but a couple of years later, caused a feeling of inadequacy as I was told that the blowjob I had given when I was 12 was so bad it "caused him to be gay."

I had two seven-year relationships, which both ended with engagement and me calling off the weddings, and a 14-year marriage, which is now ending in divorce. During my marriage, I vowed/threatened that if I ever were in a relationship again, it would only be with a woman.

It wasn't until I was in counseling in 2020 that I fully acknowledged that I was bi-sexual. Even though I have always found women attractive, trying to advance on two of my closest girlfriends would make this apparent (yes, they are still two of my closest girlfriends), I never would apply the label of bi-sexual to myself. Even though I would look at my gay friends and long to be a part of their group, I never woke up to the fact that I was supposed to be in their group!

As I near the finalization of my divorce, the intrigue of my future heightens. If I close my eyes, I can feel myself in her arms. She is taller than me and smells of the outdoors. She just holds me, running her fingers through my hair. I am at peace, loved for who I am and whole.

~ Carrie

Kiss Chase

I've had crushes on girls and women as far back as I can remember. I would fantasize about kissing my friends, teachers, and other girls in my community. I didn't realize that this wasn't considered "normal."

When I was 7, we played the game "kiss chase" on the school playground on a daily basis. I knew the routine; boys and girls lined up on opposite sides of the playground and ran toward and away from each other to kiss each other. One day, I boldly lined up with the boys so I could chase after and kiss the girls. One boy asked, "errrr, are you a lesbian?" I did not know what a lesbian was, so I asked him and reveled in his response. I didn't know a single other lesbian, but I knew that this was who I was. I was buzzing with excitement all day and couldn't wait for my mum to pick me up at school so I could tell her I was a lesbian.

As my mum approached the school gates, I shouted across the playground, "Mum, I'm a lesbian." She returned a look which let me know that I said something wrong. Mum asked me if I knew what a lesbian was, and I told her what I knew. She said, "Nicola, girls don't kiss girls," and that was the end of the conversation. I knew that this was something I shouldn't speak about again.

I can't remember how it started, but a girl and I used to sneak off to the toilets during lunch break to kiss. It happened regularly, and I enjoyed it. She was in the school year ahead of me and left my school to move up to high school. I felt so devastated. A couple of weeks later, we were reunited on a Brownie Camp holiday. The camp leader, Brown Owl, caught us kissing. She told us off, and I spent the rest of camp sleeping on Brown Owl's bedroom floor as punishment. I was 11.

When I was 15, I struggled emotionally. I was diagnosed with depression and self-harmed to release these feelings of not being understood. Around the same time, I went boy crazy, desperately seeking to feel something, anything, for boys. I had an on-off relationship for a couple of years with a guy. We laughed, we had sex, but I didn't feel how I wanted to. Mum told me he could stay the night whenever I wanted. I didn't want him to, so I never told him he could. I didn't want to share my entire self with him. I didn't want to wake up in the morning next to him, and it felt wrong forcing myself to try.

I was in a homophobic, religious cult when I was 17, which I got involved with because I had a crush on one of the cult members. The irony! The cult was full of girls and women who had relationships with women and came to the cult for "correcting." I was surrounded by other women who were attracted to women, while being reminded of how wrong it is. This echoed my experience of life so far.

My parents dragged me out of the cult and kept me at home for a few weeks, so I didn't run back. Having so much time alone, I reflected on my experiences thus far and I felt so angry at the adults in my life telling me who I should and shouldn't be. I logged onto my clunky old computer and found a dating website. I was filled with so much nervous energy and excitement as I started flirting with a woman for the first time. Later that week, we were meeting in a bar. I remember everything about that night. How she walked, how she smelled, what she was wearing, and how, when she walked towards me, our eyes locked. I had butterflies in my tummy and knew this was the start of something special. We kissed, we laughed, we held each other's hand, and I knew I could no longer hide my sexuality from myself. We spent that night together, and everything clicked. I now understood why lovers actually wanted to share a bed together after sex and wake up together. I felt so connected. She was amazing, and we were inseparable.

I introduced her to my parents as a "new friend," and I made up a story about how we met. One night, I forgot to take my keys with me, so I phoned my parents and asked them to leave a key under the mat. My girlfriend and I got home, the lights were off, and we started making out on the sofa. My parents were not in bed like we thought; they were actually hiding behind the curtains ready to scare us (a trick they regularly played on my brother and I). They caught us kissing and received the biggest scare. I denied it and told them we weren't kissing. They were so desperate to believe that their daughter couldn't possibility be kissing a girl, they ignored what they witnessed with their own eyes. I had only just started to accept my sexuality and was not prepared for my bubble to burst by telling them before I felt ready.

A few days later, New Year's Day 2002, I watched a talk show about seizing the moment. I knew this was my moment. I shouted out loud, "Mum, I'm a lesbian" echoing the words I had shouted across the playground 11 years prior.

Mum and I hugged, cried, talked, cried a bit more. She assured me that she loved me and always would. I felt my mum wasn't ready for my Dad to find out. A few days later, my dad came home from the pub and overheard a conversation my mum was having with her friend on her phone about my sexuality. I took a deep breath and braced myself for his reaction. My Dad said some hurtful things, went back to the pub, got even more drunk, came home, and couldn't remember our conversation when he woke up. So, I told him again. I could see the cogs turning as he remembered the events of the night before. He must have done a hell of a lot of processing in the pub. He gave me a hug, told me he loved me, and welcomed my girlfriend into our lives. I'm glad I came out when I did and how I did, although that wasn't intentional. Had I have been waiting for the "right" time, I think I would have been waiting for a long time.

I started telling my friends and wider family. With every person I told, it became easier for me to find the words. Their reactions were always so much better than I imagined they would be. I felt a little lighter with each person I told. Coming out is a process. You don't just come out once; as a lesbian in a hetero-normative society, you come out again and again. Society assumes I am a straight woman. Society doesn't think I look like a typical lesbian (whatever that means). If I refer to my partner, it's assumed this partner is male. I try to correct their assumptions as I feel that's the way to create change, but I don't always have the energy to do so.

I've never experienced a negative reaction when I've told another woman I'm gay. It has always been accepted as a fact. Some men have been curious about whether "I am sure" or ask, "how do I know?" Some think it's acceptable to offer me advice, such as suggesting I haven't met the right man yet or I haven't had the right dick. There's so much focus on sex, but relationships with women go so much deeper than sex for me and every queer woman I know. It's about forming an emotional, spiritual, physical connection AND a sexual connection with another human being. For me, this human has always been a woman.

Becoming comfortable with my sexuality has been a journey. I knew who I was when I was seven, but it got lost under layers of cultural conditioning and other people's expectations of who I should be. Society has changed so much in the past 20 years since I came out, but there's still so much further we need to go. It hurts my soul that in many countries it is still illegal to express love for someone of the same sex.

A couple of weeks ago, my beautiful, innocent seven-year-old nephew said, "Auntie Nic, I know what's wrong with you. You need to find a handsome man to kiss and marry. See, all this time you thought you were a lesbian, and you're not." His comment made me laugh and feel sad at the same time. Laughter because of how matter of fact he was about it, and sadness that within the first seven and most crucial years of his life, society had already taught him that queer love is not normal.

I've been in a couple of wonderful relationships with women, and I've been in a couple of shitty ones. My heart has been broken, and I have broken hearts. Through all the pain of coming out and the heartache of relationships, I have carried a sense of joy that I am now free and feel comfortable to be who I am.

Lesbian relationships, like other relationships, require nurturing, compassion, time, openness, commitment, and all the other ingredients that form an excellent basis for a relationship. Who I am now as a 37-year-old lesbian woman is so different from who I was when I had my first relationship with a woman 20 years ago. While accepting my sexuality, I've been on a huge personal development journey. I am learning who I am, what I need, and what I can offer. I have not met the love of my life yet, but I believe she is out there, and I can't wait to create and share a wonderful life with her.

~ Nicola Doherty

Parties, Marriage, and Secret Relationships

*Names and locations have been changed to protect the identities of those involved to the best of my ability.

I was sitting at a table at the Amazing nightclub with two friends who both wanted to date me, but whom, beauty aside, I just didn't want to date because their overt sexual desires just left me cold, when this woman with short hair and baggy club clothes caught my eye. She was beautifully and powerfully androgynous, (She's going to hate it when she finds out that I put it in writing for the whole world to read and argue that it's a lie; that she was always very feminine. But the ex-wife privileges she claims when she says things I don't want to hear, in ways I don't want to hear them, cuts both ways, and we have a long history of cutting one another unintentionally with our truths.) and vibrating with an intensity that I did not possess. Well, maybe beneath the filters and limitations that kept my truth from reaching the surface. The truth that I could not, would not, and should not share. I watched her across the bar as if the people around her did not exist, as if, for that moment in time, the universe only existed to give her a surface upon which her feet could land.

We met in person at a party sometime after that night. I wasn't sober, none of us were, and I seldom was when I was out with friends. I sat down next to her on the couch and awkwardly tried to chat with her. It did not go well and ended with her saying, "Go away, I'm waiting for someone better." I remember thinking to myself that I still wasn't performing masculinity well enough if someone like her wasn't even interested in speaking with me. I ended up spending the rest of the evening flirting with a rather large gentleman who quickly decided he wanted much more than I was willing to give. But that's another story for another time.

About a month later, I was hosting a party in my home and opened the door to find her standing there. She looked so confused.

"Why are YOU answering the door? Isn't this Shaney's place?"

It was, but only because she lived with me. After inviting her in, I went about enjoying my party and being stupid with my friends. In my own home, I'm much more comfortable and confident. At some point, I walked past her and said quietly, just above a whisper, "If you ever want to be more than just my friend, let me know." I didn't talk to her at all for the rest of the night.

We would end up dating a few weeks later. It was an interesting and confusing time. I'm going to share something else that she'll hate and call untrue. She was the masculine to my feminine. We balanced each other in the way we approached the world. She was often my protector, and I was often her peacemaker. Neither of us was honest about the roles we were playing.

Our marriage began with a proposal of, "You know I love you, right?"

But love was not enough. What she did not know was that I was hiding two truths. One, I understood but thought I could ignore if I just had the perfect life as the backdrop for the character of "Mr. Me" and one that I couldn't give a name to because I had not yet learned the language of who I was.

So, who was I, you ask?

I am a panromantic, asexual, trans woman. And I always have been. I knew when I got married that I was transgender but transitioning seemed impossible. The '90s were not welcoming. My experiences in school and being discharged under "Don't Ask, Don't Tell" were proof enough of that. What I did not understand was my panromantic, asexual self. I would not discover that language until after our divorce. But these truths would be the undoing of our marriage, despite the fact they were never given a voice.

The longer we were together, the more feminine she became, but I... I was already playing masculinity to the best of my ability. I could not act the part any better than I already was. Oh, and I can hear her now, "STOP telling EVERYONE I was not feminine when we met!" I need you all to understand that I don't share this to hurt her. I share this because it is the truth I saw and felt. It informs (acquaints) the way I interacted with her. I can no more pretend that I did not see her that way then she can pretend she saw anything other than a heterosexual man when she was with me. But anyway... I digress.

Where was I?

Oh, right. I was talking about already playing the role of "Mr. Me" as masculine as I possibly could. So, the other thing you need to know is that my panromantic, asexual side also played a significant role in the way our marriage ended.

See, I enjoyed flirting and cuddling and wanted both. But sex? Sex was just something I did just because my wife enjoyed it. She was the one that initiated sex, although she'll tell you it was just as often me. But that's because flirting and cuddling would often happen before she pulled us into the bedroom or somewhere semi-private. And here's the thing, because I didn't need sex and wasn't much interested in it, that time would become all about her.

But let's talk about how not understanding that I was panromantic added confusion and conflict to our relationship. I fall in love at the drop of a hat. And it doesn't matter what gender a person is. I fall, and I fall hard. But it would be years before I realized that I was falling in love with men. Because, hey, I'm asexual, and without sexual attraction, it's not a relationship. Right? But it was, and I had a series of monogamous male friendships. The time I devoted to these friendships would sometimes leave my wife feeling ignored.

I sooo had not learned how to love responsibly.

As I failed to live up to the man I was expected to be in our relationship and drifted in and out of monogamous, platonic friendships with men, my ex-wife began developing a relationship with a friend of mine—one who I knew to have no reservations about getting involved with married women. I tried to end it gently by no longer having him over or accepting invitations to places I knew he'd be. But he'd often turn up anyway. And so, without telling her why, I told her that I didn't want her hanging out with him.

Fuck! I handled that wrong. I was young, still. Ha! Like that's an excuse that could ever change shit.

She began seeing him alone without telling me. I knew. But I didn't have proof. And so, this unspoken truth broke wide open the distance between us until no bridge could cross it.

And I get it. The dude is very much everything a MAN is expected to be. Hell, if he hadn't been such a misogynist (damn, that's gonna get me in trouble with the ex.) I might have ended up in one of my monogamous male friendships with him. Oh, and maybe it makes sense to share that I never named these friendships as such until just a few years ago when a therapist and I were working through my experiences around them. So, none of these guys realized that I was (In my own heart and mind) in a relationship with them.

Our marriage ended with a phone call. "Are you somewhere you can pull over? There's something I need to tell you."

"Uh, sure, Dan. I guess," I said as I pulled off to the side of the highway. "What's up?'

"Matt quit."

"Okay. And?"

"He's moving back to Wyoming."

"Great. Why am I on the side of the highway right now?"

"Your wife and dog are with him."

The rest of the conversation is a blur, but I ended my workday right there on the side of the highway and drove home.

When I arrived home, the nail in the coffin of the life I had built was on the coffee table. A note. A goodbye. An apology that was nowhere close to enough to being able to stop the bleeding. I sobbed on the hallway floor until an exhausted sleep claimed me.

~ Jessica Purdy

Deep Truths

The hardest part about writing this chapter is that my story feels like it is always changing. I know where I began, but I have no idea where I'm going or how it will end. Most days are tinted with a shade of uncertainty, scribbled over with questions and confusion. I guess that is just part of the process of discovering your deepest truths; it's messy, terrifying, and once in a while, even a little exciting. The truths come in bits and pieces, never in a linear line that makes sense. One realization leads deeper to another one. And just when I think I've found myself, another call from within brings me deeper to learn even more. I don't know if the uncertainty will ever go away or if I'll ever get used to it, but I do know that living in denial and ignoring myself has felt like a very slow death and that the more I move forward and face my truths, the more alive and real I feel inside.

Somewhere in my mid-twenties I wrote in my journal, "All I want is to be the me I already am." I had no idea what that meant or who I already was; I just knew there was something deeper, something truer in my soul, a place that felt like home, like truth, like wholeness. I just turned 50 this year, and I'm still searching for the me I already am. It's been a long road, but I finally feel like I'm finding myself. I was right all those years ago; I have been here all along. I was just refusing to follow my own clues and pick up my own puzzle pieces.

My journey of sexuality began when I was three years old. I had the biggest crush on my older brother's friend, Bradley. I don't even know what I could have written at three, but I remember writing him love notes. That crush lasted for years. He would call me Sunshine, and I would blush myself into immobilizing shyness. It was a beautiful kind of love, full of magic and innocence, the feeling of being special to someone, and the childlike hope of "maybe someday."

As I got older, my crushes on boys continued. I'm a girl, and girls like boys, right? During high school, I had huge crushes on boys, but the idea of doing anything sexual with them was both gross and scary to me. I just really wanted to be next to them, hold their hands, and kiss them.

I enjoyed the few boyfriends I had. Being near them was exciting and touching them made my heart race. Kissing them felt like floating on a cloud. At the same time, I started connecting with a few of my girlfriends on a different level, really feeling connected with them and feeling in love with them. I had no reference point for girls liking girls and no words to express how I felt. In my small farming community in the late 80s, the only gay people I had heard about were men from the city, and it was considered shameful and disgusting. Little did I know at the time, but this was the beginning of my bi-romantic feelings for both men and women.

By the time I was in college, sex had become a thing that was expected with a boyfriend. It also became the thing that triggered long-forgotten trauma from the childhood sexual abuse I experienced at the hands of my brother between the ages of five and seven. Flashbacks and panic attacks made sexual encounters terrifying, yet because of my low self-esteem and desire for love and attention, I held my breath and closed my eyes until it was over, just like I had done with my brother.

During this time period, I met Jessica. She must have sensed something that I was completely unaware of—my sexual fluidity. There was something about the way she smiled at me that set butterflies loose in my stomach. We frequently talked about who we had crushes on, and she admitted she was questioning her sexuality. She was beginning to think that maybe she liked girls, and I could tell that I was one of them. Late nights in our pajamas, she would invite me to stay and snuggle in her dorm room. Lying next to her felt exciting and weird. I wondered what it would be like to touch her breasts, but I never did. I was too scared.

Shortly thereafter, I met the man I would marry. Dan was adorable, kind, and made me laugh. When he spontaneously pulled me close and kissed me at the party where we met, I felt like I was going to melt into the floor. Thirty years later, his arms are still my happy place and his lips still make me melt.

Within a few years of meeting however, I found myself more and more attracted to women. I never felt sexually attracted to them, it was more of strong pull towards them, a desire to be with and spend time with them. It was strong enough to cause me to question if I was gay. The idea scared me; I did not want to be gay! I was not homophobic, but I had always envisioned my life being married to a man and having a family. Being gay would ruin that and being bisexual never even crossed my mind as an option. Through terrified tears I told Dan about my feelings and surprisingly, he did not reject or shame me, and because I only wanted to be with him, we moved forward in our relationship, eventually getting married and having a baby.

Over time, my feelings for women mostly subsided as I focused on creating the traditional family life I had always envisioned, though the "internal pull that I had no words for" resurfaced for certain friends and women I knew. It was a strong desire to connect with them on a deep emotional level, to spend time with them and be intimate friends with them. Every time this resurfaced, I fought back the voice inside that kept screaming, "Your life is a LIE! The real you is GAY!" I kept hoping I would die before having to face this truth.

Years went by and I was doing a pretty good job of ignoring that internal voice, that is, until a young butch lesbian dropped into my life and turned my entire world upside down.

The first time I saw Katie, her everything caught my attention: confident attitude, masculine clothes, head shaved on the sides and back, hair slicked back in the middle. And the swagger! Oh, the swagger...

She was a new employee at the company I worked for and was being given a tour of the office on her first day. As she walked past my desk, something within me began to come alive. Once I figured out what department she worked in, I went out of my way to walk past her desk just so I could look at her. Even getting a glimpse of the back of her head made me swoon, and the voice that once threatened to blow my cover was now screaming inside, "Oh my God, did you see how CUTE she is?!" But this time, I did not ignore my internal voice. Instead, I decided to listen to it. My internal words were too juicy and exciting to ignore. This time, I wanted to hear more.

Maybe it was being on the edge of turning 50, or maybe it was the meditation and personal growth work I had already been doing, but this time I was determined to stop ignoring myself and face whatever there was to face. The first thing I had to do was have a talk with my husband.

Our conversation began with me saying something like, "Do you remember how I sometimes like girls?" and ended with him telling me that he knew that this was something I've struggled with for a long time, and even though he might lose me in the process, it's time for me to figure myself out. And so, with his blessing and a new-found openness to my feelings, I proceeded to feel everything. For the first time in my life, I allowed my thoughts to "go there." I allowed my curiosity to wonder what it would be like. I allowed and held space within myself for the confusion, uncertainty, terror, excitement, and even butterflies to coexist within my body at one time. I was a crazy mess on the inside!

Not to mention the way this girl made my body feel. In the past, my attractions were romantic, emotional. I had never even wanted to kiss a girl before, and suddenly that was all I could think about! And not just her lips, I wanted to kiss her all over! All these thoughts and fantasies made my armpits sweat and cause me to stutter whenever I tried to talk to her. One time, I almost bumped into her turning a corner and my entire body lit up like a Christmas tree causing my nipples to tingle with excitement. It was like my body was going through second puberty! That is some crazy shit when you're my age!

Every day after work I would tell my husband if I saw her or not and everything I was feeling. He would patiently listen and kindly allowed me to go through my process. He would even playfully tease me sometimes, joking that I probably had to grab onto her cubicle to stop because of the slippery trail of juices I was producing in her presence. I did my best to stay open and allow myself to feel any and all emotions. Some days

I cried, other days I fantasized, and still other days I felt like the uncertainty of what it all meant was going to kill me.

Was I gay? Was I meant to be with a woman?

Over time I realized I still found men attractive. I could walk down the same street and think a woman was cute and a man was hot. That's when I finally understood that I wasn't secretly gay, I was bisexual. I like BOTH men and women.

Why hadn't this ever occurred to me? Why wasn't that an option all these years? I think this is in large part to bisexuality being misunderstood and erased in society. It is frequently dismissed as a phase or believed that the person is doing it for attention. Even within the LGBTQ+ community, there can be hostility toward bisexuals, claiming that they are untrustworthy cheaters. Society prefers people in boxes they can understand, and bisexuals don't fit into either gay or straight boxes. There is also a false belief that a person's partner defines their sexuality; meaning, if a person is in an opposite-sex relationship, that means they are heterosexual. If they are in a same-sex relationship, that means they are gay. Therefore, their bisexuality is negated or erased completely. The truth is a bisexual person can be in a homo or a hetero relationship, and it doesn't change their sexuality. They are still bisexual.

So, where does all this leave me? Well, I did eventually gather the courage to talk to my co-worker. I honestly thought I was going to pass out, but I did manage to tell her that I was coming to terms with my bisexuality and I thought she was really cute. She kindly declined my unspoken invitation, saying that she doesn't have the mindset for getting involved with someone who is married, which I respect, though I would be lying if I said I wasn't disappointed.

My husband has remained steadfastly supportive. We frequently talk about my journey and the things I am learning about myself. Maybe someday threesomes will be an option, but for now, I need to experience being with a woman on my own, which he respects and supports. It's amazing that the thing I thought was going to tear us apart has actually brought us even closer together. And so, I go forward, remaining as open to my process as I can and keeping my eye out for the right person to experience my newly understood sexuality with.

~ Diane

The Rhythms Of My Life

My rhythm is bongos and steel drums, violins and cellos, guitars, big band, rock and roll, a little bit of country, and all that jazz.

My life is music, drum circles, meditative singing crystal bowls, copper Buddha bowls, wind in the trees, water flowing, and birds singing.

I live my life in color. I see movies and pictures in my head, from the room I will decorate, the craft or dress I will make, the card I will design, the life I shall live. My desires are the colors of my life, from the car I own showing up when I need it to the people and guardians I desire to know.

My desire always brings what I need, from the lifestyle I choose to the doctors I need to fix me and all the loves of my life. My passion becomes my reality, as the laws of the Universe live and work in my dreams and desires.

This rhythm shall always be from now until the end of time.

My rhythm initially was fun and laughter. I never met a stranger, and after childhood sexual abuse, it changed to mud and stone walls. My rhythm was designed to protect me from what I feared—abuse, ridicule, bullying, intimidation, rape, and disdain. I felt fear to hear my own voice, fear to thrive as a person, fear to be all that I can be, and fear of who I am. I wasn't always able to fight against my fear; instead, I let it control me. I survived abuse in all its forms, sexual, emotional, and physical. I tried to conform, to stay small, and to remain within the boundaries of society's expectations. I chose sex, drugs, and alcohol as my way to cope. I tried marriage to a monster, twice, which perpetuated my belief that I was unworthy, that I was terrible, and that I was merely wrong somehow.

My rhythm was pure hell in the second divorce, dirtier and longer than any in the county's history. The courts appointed a psychologist to evaluate the both of us. After the evaluations, she told me it was best to stop fighting for our children's custody because he would end up killing us all if I did not. This sage advice was not the first time I had heard it from a professional. The abuse, the disdain, the emotional demands over many years and two marriages to the same man took such a toll on me that I had to stop the madness. I decided to remove myself from the equation and move to Miami, Florida. I had hoped this would save us all; it did not, and my children and I paid a considerable price. However, I still believe the cost would have been higher had I remained in Ohio.

My rhythm of life changed and grew after spending time in Miami and the Caribbean, as I found that I always showed up no matter where I went. Try as you might, you can never hide from your true self. I made a conscious choice to work on myself, learn to be real, live in the moment, throw the rearview mirror away, and face the future with eyes wide open. Eventually, I found my voice, my purpose, my tribe, and the true me. I discovered that I have great courage. I could endure, and I am strong. Fear only needs to give me pause to stop and decide the path to take. It no longer needs to control me if I choose not to let it. I began to fill my toolbox with all the tools I could, from gratefulness, forgiveness, kindness, and love, no matter the time or distance. I then added a dash of the shaman's way, a massive number of animal totems, lots of chakra healing, deep meditation, and tarot card mastering.

Finally, I topped off the toolbox with a setting of intentions, rituals, and listening to the voice of my goddess.

My rhythm is teenagers, wild and crazy, scary and pushy, righteous and demanding, judgmental and loving while becoming the parent I had never gotten. When I chose to move back to Ohio, I focused on parenting my three teens—two daughters and my son. It was not an easy decision, nor was it perfect. Leaving Miami was bittersweet, losing love, changing my focus once again, keeping some lifetime friends, and losing others. In Ohio, I still had challenges to face in my personal life. I dated some but found my choices in partners again wanting, so I made more time for the many challenges I had ahead of me. Learning to be a parent to my children and a productive part of society was difficult enough without the added judgment of my ex and my children's friends and their parents. Then came the loss of my business, and I began to falter and forget what to do in the face of adversity.

My rhythm evolved to sadness, grief, and piety. I forgot my toolbox, and as the years waned, so did my connection to the source. I went on a sabbatical of sorts for a few soul-searching years. I lived on my own, alone, and I invariably grew to enjoy my own space and time. Having the children became my only pleasure and also my pain.

My rhythm was finding FUN, life was but a game, and I was a kid in a candy store. I changed careers and went to work for an airline as a customer service rep working the counter and gates. I loved the job more than any other I'd had to date. But soon, money grew tight, so I took on a fabulous male airline employee as my roommate. We lived together for almost a year, during which 9/11 happened. Everything changed, and the airline job grew vastly different. My roommate moved on to work for the newly formed TSA in Florida. I stayed on with the airlines, getting a promotion to an SSR, a special service rep.

My rhythm of optimism allowed me to enjoy the tasks of helping irate and disabled passengers, which was almost heaven for me. As well, I became the Airline HUB, threat trainer. Part of that position included inspecting every plane before they went out with passengers. During a galley check on one of our Airbus 320 aircraft, this woman stepped on board. She was the airline liaison for food delivery. I remember her looking me up and down as she began to flirt incessantly with me. I laughed and teasingly asked her if she was flirting with me; she, of course, just grinned and denied any such thing.

My rhythm was speaking my mind, not backing down, and making the customers happy while maintaining my customer service honor. In contrast, my future wife worked downstairs with baggage and airplane capacity loads. Over the next few months, we serendipitously ended up in the same places simultaneously, always meeting on the tarmac or at the gates as planes came and went. After a month of that, we just started meeting for breaks, food, or a smoke. Most of the crew that worked downstairs knew me as "Sparky," which is where I would spend the vast majority of my time since upstairs, they knew me as that "BITCH Kristin." I developed a bit of ego with my promotion, and it ended in a disaster of self-sabotage. Although I loved what I was doing, I let the naysayers ruin it for me.

My rhythm of life was fun and carefree, and my responsibilities became enjoyable. I was still dancing to my own beat, dating as a pastime, not an end game. I was pretty casual with my relationships and had a few different partners. One such partner was a pilot, who apparently had a steady girlfriend, unbeknownst to me. The girlfriend happened to be a favorite among the other gate crew, and I became the BITCH. I lived it proud on the outside while internally feeling small.

My rhythm in casual sex included a beautiful black man, and I liked him well enough but never felt serious about him in any way. He suddenly decided to ask me to marry him, as he wanted a child of his own. I thought about it for a quick second, but instead of agreeing, I told him we needed to be a bit more serious about our relationship. Maybe try actual dating for a while before we talked about marriage.

My rhythm was dancing in the rain, taking care of my children, and living life to the fullest. My rhythm was also contemplation. The day after he asked me, I was downstairs on the tarmac smoking a cigarette, thinking about the offer. I had wanted to get remarried someday and maybe have another child, so the possibility intrigued me. As I looked out over the tarmac and runways contemplating life, I suddenly felt the presence of someone behind me and a tap on the shoulder. I screamed a little as I jumped out of my skin. But when I turned around, she gave me this look, which I have now seen many times over the years, questioning but seeing directly into my soul. She asked me what I was so engrossed in that I hadn't realized she was there. I told her about his offer, and she said, "Okay fine, I guess that tells me all I need to know," and she turned to go. Immediately, I heard a loud and clear message in my head that said, "if you let her walk away, it will be the worst mistake of your life.

If you instead take her hand, your life will be more complete than you have ever known."

So, what else do you do when the Universe speaks, and time stands still for a moment? I reached out and grabbed her hand; I told her not to go. "I have no intention of marrying him," I said, "but I would like to spend my life with you." We agreed to a date that evening. Although I knew she was the one, I was still really nervous about our first real date, so I had one of my good friends and my roommate come with us. The date went so well for all of us; I was his best man when he married that good friend a few years later.

Our rhythm together was laughter and love; life was jobs, paychecks, and mundanity. We lived years with guilt from our past, never forgiving, always needing to rile the ups and downs of life, parenting, and caretaking. We were learning to co-exist within our pure vulnerability and true love. As the years passed, we would remember the fun we had working with the airlines. Years later, my wife bought up the girlfriend of one of the pilots that worked with us. As she told me his and her story, I started to laugh and said, you know, upstairs, I was Kristin. My wife looked at me bizarrely and said, "Wait a minute, you were the Bitch Kristin!" laughing as she said it. I said, "Yep, I was Sparky downstairs, but upstairs I was the Bitch." We laughed so hard that our bellies and faces hurt as she put two and two together.

Our rhythm together comes from the fact that love comes in many shapes, sizes, and packages. Always be open to the possibilities, and let the heart be your guide. I was not expecting my soulmate to be in a woman's body, yet I fell head over heels in love with who she is, not what she is. She had always known she was gay but came from a generation and location where she had to hide who and what she was. I came from a world that, until I was about 25, didn't even know "gay'" existed. And yet, this woman embodied all that I ever wanted in a partner. She is funny, kind, hard-shelled, fiercely loyal, accepting, nonjudgmental, unaccepting, judgmental, jealous and desirous, a great cook, and she's beautiful inside and out. She's also intelligent, a great storyteller, loves popcorn, ice cream, hikes in the woods, long nights in front of the fire, and is an amazing lover. I asked for all of that and got it. The Universe laughed but gave me my heart's desire, just like I asked. Maybe I was not expecting it in a female body. Still, I am infinitely glad I was open and comfortable enough in my own skin to accept the infinite possibilities of our union.

Our rhythm together was love, not marriage, but after my wife's work allowed for domestic partnerships, we decided on a union, alone and illegal, on top of a mountain. We exchanged Celtic knot rings in the Smoky Mountains. I am Irish and she is Syrian; knots mean a lot to both of us. Our legal union happened in 2013 at the first courthouse in America, in Queen Anne, Maryland. But alas, not all love is bliss; sometimes, the Bitch wants to play, feelings get hurt, opinions get ignored, and hearts get laid open. Sometimes it's an accident or a disease that changes everything. We become caretakers instead of lovers, but laughter and less seriousness is our game, and even when we are angry, we laugh to lighten the load. Love brings extreme and exhilarating joy if you allow the love to be pure, real, and fun.

Our rhythm is adventures through backroads, canyons, and dust. We lived on byways, highways, and fast freeways. But, the beckoning of the ocean, the crash of the waves, and the sunsets were always calling us home. Waiting long for the law to catch up with our hearts, yet never fully believing. Together forever, for better or worse, in sickness and in health, so shall we always be. With proper care, romance ebbs and flows, love builds and grows, but laughter and communication are the secret tricks.

My rhythm was never labeling. I had never felt gay or straight because labels are so unnecessary. Sex is for pleasure, no right or wrong. So, I enjoyed sex throughout my life with both men and women. But, when my soul recognized her soul, I felt something so right, so perfect with her. We have been inseparable for almost 20 years now. Some years were comfortable, some exciting, and some years way harder than we thought they could ever be. She is my heart, my soul mate, my friend, and sometimes my caretaker, but most of all, she is always the love of my life.

My rhythm has been a journey in love, in pain, in delight, in bitchiness, in anger, in magic, in mindfulness, in humility, and in endurance, courage, and strength, all of it finding my way back to my truth. Just as I call each challenge from my cosmic library, I, too, call my healing, my tribe, and my heart. I have had to learn not to question the how, but only to believe the Universe has my back. I have had to discover that each challenge was a lesson to be learned or repeated until completed. And if we, in this life, play our cards right, and into that good night, we will brawl and crawl, for a life well-lived and well-loved is the best life of all.

~ Kristin Sparks

Mook's Story

I don't know why I didn't realize it as a child. I don't know why I didn't see it as a young adult. I don't know why I didn't realize I was a lesbian until I was 50 years old. Growing up, being interested in someone of the same sex was a no-no. If you saw two women walking together holding hands, someone was bound to whisper, "They're gay," as if it was a bad thing. I would look away, knowing that was something you didn't want to be. But, as I got older and would fantasize about being with a partner, sexually, it was always with another woman. I thought that was normal. I mean, I had female parts, and I knew what felt good, so of course I would think about being intimate with a woman. I figured once I was finally with a man, I'd fantasize about the male anatomy.

Yeah, right.

I didn't have sex with a man until I was with my first husband, right before we were married. I hadn't even kissed anyone before him. I hated it. He was a selfish lover, and it was only about pleasing him, which could literally take hours. In the dark, I would cry as he had me pleasure him. Although, that really wasn't what I did. He constantly told me I was doing things wrong and wouldn't let me rest. He never pleased me.

Not once.

Fast forward to that marriage ending (for many reasons) and I was left thinking that he was the reason I didn't enjoy sex. Then I met another man; he would become husband #2, and sex with him was better. He did try to please me, but only the way he wanted. We had two kids, and for many years, sex was an obligation, only when he made me feel guilty for not having it. After many years, I asked to try new things, but he said I was too aggressive. I couldn't win! When we did have sex, it was mostly to get him off. Then, I'd have to clean him up and he'd fall asleep. I'd go take a shower and cry. Thank goodness for my vibrator! I'd have a little fun once he was at work and the kids were at school.

Being a voracious romance reader, I would gobble up books. I read almost all day. I was severely depressed, so much so, that my doctor told me she was out of medication options and she might need to find me more drastic treatments. The books would transport me to a happier place. One day, I discovered lesbian romance books, and they became my dirty little secret. Unfortunately, my husband had access to my downloaded book titles, so while I didn't read them a lot, I would get very turned on when I did. But I just could not understand why. I mean, I'm married to a man. How can two women turn me on?

Then, one day I found the term bi-curious and I thought that's what I must be. I found a website with women chatting about their interest in other women, and they claimed to be bisexual. That's what I am, I thought. I made friends with some of these women and some of them liked to write erotic stories with each other. I joined in and found I had a talent for it. Writing became my new way to escape. Having no sexual experience with a woman, I found I could just write about what I'd fantasized about. I enjoyed this sharing of stories, but I wanted it to be real. I met another woman on this site, and we became friendly. We messaged each other through this site. She gave me her phone number so we could text and not go through the site anymore. I had taken a screenshot of her phone number, so I'd have it to input into my contacts. This screen shot also had the name of the website in it. Unbeknownst to me, my husband had all of my photos going to a central place with his, so he saw this phone number with a text from her, and a strange website. He cornered me about it, and I started to make up some excuse and finally just thought, what the heck, I'll tell him. I said, I like women. I'm bisexual. The truth was, I hadn't been happy in my marriage for years. There was control. Him over me. My therapist said we'd always had a parent/child relationship. Plus, I hadn't been happy in years, period! He didn't really accept that I was bisexual. I don't blame him. To him, it came out of nowhere. It seemed like that to me too.

One day, he said if you were fully gay, I think I could understand it more than you being a bisexual. I gave that a lot of thought and I did some research. I began to understand that I actually identified more with being gay than being bisexual. From the day I accepted that I was a lesbian, my life changed. I was no longer depressed and no longer binge eating. That is not to say that it has all been a bed of roses since that revelation. My husband still couldn't accept it. He would not accept an open relationship. I told him that if I ever meet a woman I fell in love with, I'd want the opportunity to be with her.

He didn't hear me. He embarked on a mission to "win me back." He was attentive in ways he hadn't been for years. He bought me things. I told him more than once about leaving if I met anyone.

Then, I met someone.

I fell hard. She flew out to visit. She was the first female I'd ever kissed. I finally understood what those fireworks everyone talks about are like. The kisses led to more, and in her arms, I finally felt like I was home. After a week, I told my husband I was in love with this woman, my girlfriend. Thus began 10 months of guilt, anger, sadness, and regret. He didn't kick me out. I had no money of my own; I stopped teaching when we had kids, 13 years earlier. We were civil. The kids had no idea, but it was tense.

Fourteen months later, I suffered a stroke. Yes, my husband took care of me. My guilt grew and grew. Then Covid hit and now we've been together 24/7 for 10 months I still have my girlfriend. We haven't seen each other in person in over a year. My husband knows she's still in my life. We don't talk about her.

I've taken the past year to reflect and learn about the real me to answer the questions I've been asking myself and seeing signs that pointed to my sexuality long before I realized it. I don't know how to move forward with causing my husband more pain. He's not a bad person. Just not the person for me. I am glad I finally figured out who I am, and although it's been a difficult journey for me and I've caused pain, I know I'm still on this exciting, crazy journey. I'm happy to be on the path to being my truest self.

~ Mooks (Deana)

Katie: Amazing Gays and Twas the Night

Fifteen years ago, I married into a very musical family. My husband's sister sang at the Vatican for the Pope, they sang at church, they sang around the dinner table, literally, they sang everywhere. Imagine one of those Southern Baptist traveling family groups; it was like that. They are very talented. Me, not so much. I auditioned for the role of Ariel in my school's production of "The Little Mermaid" and I got the part of stage crew. Not even Mermaid #3 or the chorus. No, they were just like "Wear black, go backstage, and shhh!"

So, when I got engaged, my mom was worried that I wouldn't fit in. She asked, "Do they know about you?"

And no, no they didn't. Turns out there was a lot they didn't know about me.

I came out a few years ago to pretty much everyone else and decided it was time they know too. Since they were so musical, I thought I'd write a little song. But, since I don't know music,

I had to borrow someone else's song. So, I first wrote a little something to the tune of Vanilla Ice, but then I thought they're really not ready for Dyke Baby. I decided I need to speak their language, so I went with something more familiar to them. So, here's "Amazing Gays." (sing along to the tune of Amazing Grace)

Amazed I'm gay
but they shouldn't be,
although I married a dude
I love Indigo Girls
Roller Derby
I drive a Subaru
But I was taught that gay is sin
And sin would send me to hell,
So, I spent thirty-five years
trying to be straight
And I faked it pretty well. (fooled all their asses)
Through many counselors
Books and prayers
I finally came to see,
There's nothing fucking wrong with me,
Or my sexuality
So here I am,
Out free and proud
Haters can take a hike,
My rainbow gear
will make it clear,
That I'm a happy dyke!
Katie: Twas the Night

I'm a very gay woman married to a very straight man. It's kind of unconventional, but it's working for us. I met a girl, went on a date. She was kind of skeptical, like how did I not know I was a lesbian? Fair. Looking back, there were so many red flags that should have tipped me off that maybe a heterosexual marriage wasn't my destiny. Like when my friends all went to see Magic Mike and they walked outta there all hot and flustered and I was like "Do you think those guys focused on weights or cardio to get in shape?"

But then when Hustlers comes out, I'm like "woo hoo!" and they're all "eww, that's offensive to women." And, I said, "Okay, you need to not look at my browser history," I'm pretty sure PornHub isn't gonna meet your standards. And then I had to rethink who I would assign in my will to clear my computer.

Do you have that friend? That person you can trust in the case of an emergency to go in and delete your history and any incriminating evidence?

When I was in college, I learned that I was not that friend.

My roommates didn't think I could handle their porn stash. They said I was too sweet and innocent, and they didn't want to corrupt me.

I was offended for a minute, because deep down I wanna be a badass and wear leather jackets and have tattoos. But they were right. I am not a badass. I'm a preschool teacher. I get paid to sing and wipe noses and remind my little friends to use their big boy words.

But, due to Covid, I have not been able to hang out with my little friends in a really long time and I miss them. I miss the songs and the stories. So, I decided that tonight I'm going to read y'all a story. Let's get settled in.

The first thing we're going to do is get all our wiggles out. Do this with me.

I wiggle my fingers, I wiggle my toes, I wiggle my ears, I wiggle my nose. Now that all the wiggles are out of me, and I can sit quietly, as quietly as can be.

Now you all may have heard of "'Twas the Night Before Christmas." This is kinda like that. But it's about Miss Katie, and the night of my first date.

'Twas the night of my first date with the first girl I met
I thought I was gay, but wasn't sure yet
I bought brand new undies, a black lacey pair
Not my Fruit of the Loom granny underwear
My husband settled in for a long night alone
When I grabbed my purse and my keys and my phone
He looked up and asked me how late I'd be
I said I love you, don't wait up for me please!
I raced out of the house and he raised one eyebrow
No seriously, I said, I'll see you tomorrow!
My GPS took me straight to the place where we'd meet
I pulled up to the door, she jumped in the front seat.
She had tight jeans and boots and an ass that won't quit
I knew that this night was gonna be it.
With a twinkle in my eyes, some smooth talk and luck
This is the night we would finally...
Hung out at a bar, we joked, and we flirted
We stayed there so late, the whole place was deserted.
Enough of this chit chat, I grabbed her, let's go
I've got something to prove, something I need to know.
Back to our hotel room and I bolted the door
pulled back the covers, dropped clothes to the floor
Faster than fireworks how quickly I came,
I whispered and shouted and called out her name
Now harder, and faster, just like that, right there
People could hear me, and I didn't care!
So up rose my body, my muscles grew tight
I clutched at the sheets as I yelled in delight
And then in a twinkling I just laid on the bed

"I didn't know it could be like that!" I said.
I took a deep breath, gulped down some water
She stood up to get dressed but I quickly caught her
She was gorgeous and blonde with curves in just the right place
Tattoos on her skin that my lips wanted to trace
Her eyes, how they twinkled. Her smile was inviting
My own bottom lip I couldn't stop biting
Her body was epic, a true goddess in form
One night with this woman and I felt reborn
A wink in my eye and then in the quiet
I had an idea, and decided to try it
I flipped her around, said "Now you're my bitch"
Thought I was a bottom, turns out I'm a switch!
My theory was tested, hypothesis true
What I expected, what I always knew
My attraction to men was culturally formed;
I followed the rules to fit into the norm.
But when I gave myself the freedom to choose
I just wanted a WAP with some sexy tattoos!
~ Katie

I Kissed a Girl and I Liked It

Many years ago, when I was married to a man, I fell in love with a girl named Serena. Serena van der Woodsen.

Okay, I fell in love with Blake Lively in Gossip Girl.

Whatever.

At the time, I just assumed everyone was in love with her. Look at her, for crying out loud. In the back of my mind, I wondered if I was sexually attracted to women.

Fast forward to this summer and an event suggestion surfaced on social media for a Lesbian Pop-up Bar. Color me intrigued. Madison didn't have an official lesbian bar, so an organizer created the event to take over a specific bar for the evening. As an ally, I proudly wore a shirt declaring, Love is Love with Wonder Woman and Supergirl kissing each other. I didn't need to be a card-carrying lesbian to pop into the event, right?

I arrived at the bar to find no signage. What was I supposed to do? Walk up to a table and ask, "Hey, are you the lesbians?"

Instead, I walked up to the bar and found an old friend bartending. We hadn't seen each other in years, not since our sons were in elementary school together. After the usual quick pleasantries, and not in the mood to make small talk, I scurried off to the bathroom where I texted his ex-wife about my adventure. She found my whole situation amazing.

Having driven a half-hour to be there, I wasn't going to give up so easily, but I needed time to figure out what I was going to do. Leaving the bathroom, I returned to my friend at the bar, and he asked who I was meeting there.

Here went nothing. "Do you know where the pop-up bar is?"

Bless his heart, he must have been so confused. Last he knew, I was definitely married to a man. But he didn't bat an eye when he pointed behind me. "I think it's that table over there."

He was right, and I met a fabulous group of ladies. Victoria really intrigued me. She wore a vintage dress and hairstyle and had a beautiful smile.

As the conversations died down, I was ready to head home. I thanked everyone at the table for a lovely evening and stopped by the bar to say goodbye to my friend.

Victoria came up to pay her bill, and we walked out together. Before we got to our cars, I asked for her phone number. Not having dated since high school, was that even how it worked now? I guessed so. She gave it to me.

The next day, I flew out of town for a work conference. Being an extrovert and working from home the last six years was an interesting combination. I'd become close with several colleagues, and time with them in real life was a dream. The last time we'd had a conference like that had been two weeks after my wedding.

It was very surreal to be with my co-workers once again with my marriage being over. Some knew. Many didn't. There wasn't really an appropriate social media post for everything that had happened, so I told colleagues in person. But only if they asked about my personal life. It was actually freeing to tell my former boss, who still sat in our weekly virtual staff meeting.

As a visual learner, I appreciated the signs in our conference room.

Be Genuine

Be Remarkable

Be Worth Connecting With

I vowed to be all of those as I watched the rain on my way to the airport. As I looked out the plane window, a rainbow was ready to take me home.

Back home, I texted Victoria and asked if she'd like to get coffee. We met a week later and chatted for hours. It was easy conversation, as we both had teenagers very close in age. I mentioned the drag show that night.

"I love drag," she said.

The next day, I asked her if she'd like to join me at a drag show that week. Done and done. Dating a woman is easy. We had a great time at the show, and my friends approved of her.

After a few more texts back and forth, I asked if she was looking forward to Pride weekend because I was.

I never heard from her again. Maybe dating a woman wasn't so easy after all.

Fast forward three months. I raced into my favorite night-club, excited to start my weekend, see my friends, and watch a drag show. I said hello to Derrick, his cousin, and their friend, Quinn. I'd met both of them at Derrick's fundraiser the month before. I hugged everybody and told them, "Nice to see you again."

Later in the evening, I wanted to dance. I happened to be near Quinn. "OMG, I love this song. Let's dance!" And off we went. After a little bit, she asked, "You want a shot?"

"Why not?" A friend of Derrick's was a friend of mine, right?

Two days later, I was back to finish off my Sunday Funday. Derrick and company were there again. I decided to go for it—when Derrick was alone. "Does Quinn like girls, boys, or everybody?" I asked him.

"Well... she's actually experimenting right now."

"Okay. Well, I'm asking for a reason."

"Then you should come sit at the bar with us."

I walked over with Derrick and started chatting with the group.

After a little while, Quinn asked a loaded question. "Jaimie, do you come up to Appleton not for fundraisers?"

"I could."

Derrick almost spit out his entire drink.

Minutes later, I headed to the bathroom. On my way out, I saw Quinn walking in my direction. I specifically say not toward me because she was in a main crossroads in the bar and could have been going to the bathroom, going outside, or going to the dance floor. So, I asked her. "Hey, where are you going?"

"I was going to the bathroom to make out with you."

About face. And there I was. Since nothing physical had ever happened with Victoria, it was my first time really kissing a female. And I liked it. And yes, I heard the Katy Perry song in my head too.

~ Jaimie

Feels Like Home

I met her at the gym before a fitness class and there was just something about her that felt so familiar and comfortable. As we connected, she was so genuine and not afraid to show her true self to me. I found this to be magnetic, and it made me feel safe to show myself to her too. It was a side of me that previously, no one could see because of my fear and shame.

I had been brought up in a loving but strict, right-wing house where my sister and I were trained to be good Christian kids. I wasn't allowed to listen to mainstream music because of the evil messages, had to always be polite, not watch "inappropriate" TV shows (like "Three's Company"), go to church, and obey my parents or face certain punishment. I learned that in order for me to be acceptable, I had to morph into someone that I was expected to be. So, when I found my preteen self being sexually attracted to girls, I thought I was truly deviant. Nevertheless, I would often sneak off to watch contraband sexy music videos at my friends' houses.

When I was 12 years old, I started coming up with "sexy games" at my sleepovers which involved dares where there was skin flashing, touching, licking, etc., and I remember feeling really achy "down there." I was tormented by lustful thoughts of women's bodies and would try to sneak peeks in Cosmopolitan magazine for perfume ads which occasionally involved at least one partially naked breast (sometimes, there would even be a jackpot nipple!). However, by the time I was of dating age, even though I was so attracted to females, I followed my conditioned upbringing and only dated boys. I wrapped my head around this by telling myself I only found women sexually attractive, but I could never be IN LOVE with a woman, therefore, I am not gay. Kissing a woman would just be too weird. This is how I reconciled the "evilness" within me. At 19, I got married to a man. A man who loved me very much but unfortunately had a sex addiction, which led to him straying outside of the marriage many, many times. We ended up deciding to cohabitate to raise our children together but were not intimate (physically or emotionally). We were friends and roommates.

Ten years into this cohabitation, I met her. When I spoke to her, it felt safe, like I was talking to myself! The more open I was, the closer we got, and this new-found intimacy which I had never shared with another human, took on an irresistible life of its own. We were very close friends for almost a year, when one day I was driving to her house and noticed how fast my heart was beating. It felt like I was going to see someone I was … IN LOVE with! Over the next few months, we started to share our feelings with each other, and it was very mutual. Even though we hadn't crossed the line physically, the chemistry was off the charts!

Jumping forward to today for a moment, I have been doing a lot of self-development over the last few months, and looking back, I can see how this beginning was so intense because I was drinking up this new-found freedom to be authentic. After living for 38 years, pretending to be someone who others expected me to be, I hung on and soon found myself madly in love but deeply challenged.

We couldn't get enough of each other's presence. One night, we met in a parking lot, and she was going to tell me that we had to stop whatever this was. Those words never left her lips because she kissed me instead. Our first kiss. Was it weird and awkward like I always thought it would be? NO! It was magical in every way, and I couldn't stop kissing her from the depths of my soul. It felt like drinking the most thirst-quenching drink imaginable when you have been parched in a desert your entire life.

We started a passionate relationship. Within just three months, she left her abusive husband (which she needed to do anyway) and moved into her own house three blocks from me, so we could see each other more easily. Internally, I actually wanted to follow and move in with her so we could start a life together. Something was stopping me. I was STUCK!

I was terrified of having to tell my parents that, not only was I gay, but I was breaking my sacred marriage vows, blowing up my family, and abandoning my innocent children. This was not going to be okay. My mother was always in my business, telling me what I was doing wrong in life, or praising me for doing something she felt was right. I always felt like I didn't have control over my own choices. Meanwhile, I told my "husband" (is there another word for co-parenting roommate?) about my attraction to women and explained that I wanted to explore this. In return, he had permission to hook up with as many women as he wanted (which he was kind of doing anyway). I thought that maybe this could be a win-win, where I get to be in a beautiful relationship with the woman I loved without having to face the anguish of my parents (which I realize sounds crazy as I am an adult after all) or make my children suffer from the pain of a broken home, only seeing each parent part-time. As a mother, I didn't want to cause pain in my children's lives. We were on the same page and thought "this" could work, at least for the time being.

So, "this" continued for seven years. I experienced euphoric highs that I never dreamed possible on this earth and had new experiences that I will always treasure. But I also suffered being torn in half, unable to commit to either life and always hurting one side or the other whenever I had to make a choice. I hated being the bad guy; regardless of what I chose, someone always got hurt. I desperately wanted to be fully "out" with her so we could have a real life together. I wanted to spend Christmas with her, call her my wife, always be there for her when she needed me, and not have to hide the relationship. Over the years, more and more trusted people were told about us, but not many were supportive because they saw the dead end coming because of our enmeshed situation. If we didn't move forward together authentically, there would eventually be a breaking point, and we would shatter.

Things had gotten ugly from extreme mutual codependency. Lies, broken promises, betrayals, lashing out, hiding things from each other, temporary breakups, health issues, resentment ... all because we had found ourselves in an incredibly unsafe, toxic, and dysfunctional relationship. Four months into the Covid-19 lockdown, it finally happened. She ended it on July 23rd. I went into a tailspin.

I ended up telling my parents about the relationship because they could see that something was dreadfully wrong, and they were afraid for my life. They said they still loved me, but I knew they still did not condone same-sex relationships. My "husband" picked up the pieces and took on the brunt of the house/childcare work while I was tormented with grief. My sister was my emotional lifeline during those dark days. I wept every day for several weeks, sometimes convulsing with shock, both from detoxing from the relationship and from drowning in endless grief.

I realized that I needed to do something. I had to take these devastating emotions and channel them into self-healing. I poured myself into reading up on anything I could find that might help me. I researched codependency, attachment styles, shadow work, reparenting your inner child, and started to see progress. I was taking care of myself, joined some online support groups, I was journaling, meditating, made a choice to lose 100 lbs. (I had lost 64 lbs. and counting at the time I wrote this) and started to heal. I met some beautiful souls through this process and formed a sisterhood of support.

I started taking courses on healing my attachment style, letting go of resentment, learning how to reprogram my unhealthy core beliefs, and truly find peace and love inside of myself instead of looking for it outwardly. I had continued contact with my ex because we own a business together, and we didn't want work to be awkward. In time, we slowly became friends again, but this time it was different. It wasn't the same desperate, enmeshed type of relationship. It felt like we respected each other as individuals again.

She started to notice some changes in me (such as the way I would react to situations, my ability to communicate effectively, setting and respecting boundaries, taking responsibility for my part in what went wrong, not meddling and trying to control other people via codependent strategies, getting healthy etc.) and as our friendship started over, it bloomed for the first time into a healthy dynamic. She started taking self-development courses too because she saw what a difference it was making for me, and she also started to take responsibility for her part in what went wrong.

We still love each other, and I know that we always will. But we also agree that we can't be together the way things were before, with one foot in my marital home for the world to see and the other foot with my love in secret. So, for now, we hang out as friends, exercise together, work here and there, and encourage each other in our individual journeys toward self-development. The healthier our relationship to ourselves becomes, the more I see hope for a future again. Maybe there is a chance for us after all.

Every morning, I read a daily meditation, and today's (from Melody Beattie) said, "We do not have to feel guilty about finding happiness and a life that works. And we do not have to take on our family's issues as our own to be loyal and show we love them."

I love her. I still can feel her first kiss on my lips. I see love in her eyes when she looks at me and it glows from within. I have been rebuilding myself for six months, yet my love for her is still there ... and our love is still there. We have declared it to each other. With all these changes and using helpful tools from various resources, maybe we can both get to a place where we can put the pain from our past behind us, learn to heal, forgive each other, be brave, and for the first time, be in a truly authentic and healthy relationship where we are each responsible for our own individual emotions. I am so scared. But I am also so strong and getting stronger each day. I am excited, I am nervous and most of all, I am hopeful for the future. I have always said that her arms feel like home to me. They still do. I am finally on my way home.

~ Julie

Jennifer's Story

I am a 41-year-old mother of two, married for 21 years to a man who I met when I was 17. I grew up in a small town in central Canada in a Mennonite farming family that valued the work ethic, self-sacrifice, and the optics of perfection over honoring one's authentic self. He grew up in a small farming community on the West coast to a slightly more liberal Mennonite family, which meant that we both brought a level of naivete and sexual repression to our relationship.

I never felt that I fit in during my youth. The church we attended was extremely uncomfortable to me, and I felt constantly at odds with the teaching I was offered. I did not know what it meant to be gay, but I remember getting in a heated argument with someone in my early teen years defending the LGBT community before I really understood what that meant. Dating didn't interest me, and yet somehow, when I was fifteen, I was coerced into an emotionally abusive relationship with a 21-year-old man who informed my early sexual experiences, all without consent. It felt expected that I date a man, and because he was pursuing me, I did not feel that I had a choice. No one in my life seemed to find this to be problematic. He wanted me to drop out of school and marry him, and when I turned 16, I mustered up the strength to leave him, even though he threatened to kill himself if I did. It was terrifying, and I felt certain I would never date again. I also felt certain that I needed more than anything to get out of my small town, which was suffocating me in ways that I didn't fully comprehend. Getting out felt like a matter of life and death.

When I graduated at 17, my parents wanted me to attend a liberal bible college in the closest city to us. While the idea of bible college terrified me, I felt this was my best option for moving out of my town and into the city with some support, so based on this, I agreed to go for one year. That was where I met my husband. He was also trying to get out of his small-town upbringing and was entirely non-threatening in presence in a very opposite way to the man I had been with in high school. In fact, the day we met, he and another young man on campus introduced themselves while holding hands, and I believed them to be a couple! I was so relieved that this bible college was so openly accepting of gay couples that I was immediately drawn to the man I came to marry. I soon realized they were not, in fact, a couple, and were just being goofy 18-year-old guys, but interestingly, the other friend of that pair did come out as his authentic self after college graduation three years later. And the man who became my husband became very interested in me. He had a very slight build and a more androgynous way about him that made me feel safe. We became inseparable from that point forward, and I felt that he was my life preserver from the life I had fled because I was drowning.

We always described our relationship as a deep friendship. When we met, I didn't understand anything about my own sexuality, and my only experiences had been extremely trau-matic. He was patient and kind, and I started to connect to my body in ways that had never been possible for me. We had an enthusiastic physical relationship, but sex before marriage was a strong taboo for me, so conventional intercourse was off the table as far as I was concerned. Three years into the relation-ship, we decided to marry (even though we were total babies!) for pragmatic reasons, mostly. Living together without being married was outside of the realm of possibility and living sepa-rately didn't feel possible.

So, we got married and naively thought that sex would happen naturally and enthusiastically. And that's where it all started to unravel—because it didn't. I had a major "block," and the tension around this block started on our wedding night and grew over the course of 20 years. I believed myself to be bro-ken. I felt it was my responsibility to ensure sex happened often enough to meet his needs (which were strong and frequent), regardless of my feelings on the matter. I allowed sex to happen and was mostly only able to get past my blocks through alcohol, and then, only some of the time. We fought about it, and my anxiety and depression became almost unbearable. The guilt and shame became an immense burden, and our conversations around trying to fix the problem culminated in an emotional shutdown on my part, and ultimately, a bout with pneumonia in 2018 that hospitalized and almost killed me. I struggled with suicidal ideation and came to believe my entire value was being measured by my ability to offer sex, and in the absence of that ability, the world was better off without me.

This breaking point felt necessary to come to the realiza-tion that my identity is complex and valid. A year ago, through continual conversations and the support of therapists, we have concluded that I am a queer/questioning/possibly lesbian on the asexual spectrum (a demisexual if you will). This has validated my experience immensely and has been life-preserving; however, I am still at an extremely tentative point in terms of embracing this knowledge and granting myself permission to fully step into myself. I have my partner's full support, but we also both acknowledge that many years of damage (and non-consensual sex) have been sustained. He is committed to supporting this journey, and we are committed to staying together as I explore this aspect of myself. I continue to struggle with finding my voice and with anxiety and depression, but every step we take toward acknowledging myself brings me closer to silencing those demons.

My Next Husband Will Be a Lesbian
Pasha Marlowe

I knew walking down the aisle, didn't you?

I did what I thought I was supposed to do.

I found the guy, fell in love, and said yes.

I bought the white dress, ordered the roses, and picked out the china.

I linked arms with my dad for the first and last time in my life.

I posed in the church, looking over my shoulder for the photos.

I wore the high-heeled shoes and pantyhose.

I even had a fucking sailboat ice sculpture.

I don't even like boats ... or churches ... or watching weddings anymore.

I convinced myself and others that I was settled.

I celebrated being accepted into a new extended family.

I ignored the constant betrayals and lies and the voices that tried to warn me.

I escaped my own knowing by immersing myself in books about the psyche.

I protected myself by sculpting a body of thick armor.

I taught yoga to feign contentment and as an attempt to quiet my thoughts.

I birthed two phenomenal children who became the glue.

I hid behind the portrait of an unbroken family for 14 years.

I tried to forgive again and again, until I couldn't breathe, despite the yoga.

I numbed the grief of co-parenting by seeking love and sex.

I got pregnant again through the sex, go figure.

I told the father, and he seemed pleased.

I figured we should marry, to keep everything tidy.

I pretended not to care that we skipped the proposal and ring bit.

I borrowed a blue dress to accommodate my growing belly.

I walked down the aisle alone that time, not in a church, but in a barn covered in bat poop.

I asked for sunshine, but the universe brought rain to conceal my tears.

I put on a brave smile for myself and my kids, who sang during the ceremony.

I replaced the ice sculpture with a labyrinth, which just made me dizzy, and ended me up right where I started, with another child who makes my soul sing and another man I can't fully trust.

And a voice that keeps saying, "I want more."

I am 14 years into my second "good enough" marriage.

I delight in my three children who allow the world to make sense.

I enjoy work that aligns with my purpose and passion to heal.

I own an adorable house in a scenic town near the ocean.

I have a car, enough money, and a Cavapoo puppy.
I even have the proverbial white picket fence.
I have a white, heteronormative, cisgendered, privileged life.
I can't think of a reason to complain, except my husband's affairs keep happening and
I no longer feel safe in my own body and
I can't sleep and
I am angry and
I am lonely, even though my house is crowded.
I have glimpses of me belonging.
I rejoice with my friends who call each other goddesses.
I witness myself sharing and loving freely.
I catch myself spontaneously dancing and singing.
I hear myself laughing and lusting.
I recognize the fire still inside.
I imagine the softness of a woman's curves.
I remember what I tried for decades to forget.
I sense my body cracking open and the light pouring in
I allow myself to dream of womanhood beyond motherhood.
I am not simply a portal.
I greet myself at my own front door*.
I delight in the view.
I lock eyes with her.
I fantasize about warmth and wetness.
I rise with pleasure.
I long to be worshipped.
I desire.
I am flying ...
I crash land.
I know better than to leap from my nest.
I have a husband who tucks me in at night, goes grocery shopping, and catches mice.

I have a sweet kid who I still picture swinging between our arms.

I have future plans, though they are starting to look cloudy.

I have security but am tired of feeling secure.

I demand loyalty, and I want to explore.

I wish to forgive, and I wish to stop struggling.

I desire to spoon, and I desire to sleep alone.

I want to stay, and I want to go.

I want to want him, and I want to find her.

I want to feel what it's like to truly feel.

I wonder if there is a way to hold space for it all.

I am giving voice to this longing.

I am coming out from hiding.

I am certain and confused by my sexuality in every moment of every day.

I identify as a paradox ... has X been claimed yet?

I identify as worthy of love, laughter, and loyalty.

I identify as a woman who is more than she appears.

I identify as believing that bliss is in the cards for me.

I identify as someone who wants a life partner who would never choose an ice sculpture.

I imagine there won't be an aisle next time, just wide-open sky, comfortable shoes, and a feeling of coming home.

I write all this as my little boy sleeps upstairs and my husband wraps Christmas presents.

I stare at the tree, pining away over which ornaments I would choose if we were to part.

I wonder who would get the dog.

I taste the tears streaming down my face, imagining losing any time with my child.

I recall how painful it is to share holidays with an ex and to feel the old future slip away.

I believe that I want my marriage to survive these revelations.

I know I am open to creative solutions.

I am certain I can't continue as is.

I turned 50 this year.

I do not have much time left to figure life out.

I fear I am dreaming too big.

I fear I may end up alone.

I fear more a life with regret.

I don't want to die by paper cuts.

I want to die from tireless exploration and adventure.

I hold on to my intuition by the thinnest of silk threads.

I worry that if I publish these words, there will be no turning back.

I hope if I publish these words, there will be no turning back.

I am terrified.

I am curious.

I am worthy.

That feels like enough reason right now to push... s e n d.

Greet yourself at your own front door is a saying from the poem "Love After Love" by Derek Walcott

Afterward: The Trauma of the Bisexual Experience

Dr. Jamie Marich

Bisexuals are used to receiving messages—explicit and implicit—from the world around us. Many of the classics include: "There's no such thing as bisexuality," "You're just confused and trying to sort things out," and of course, "You'll have sex with anyone to get what you want." All of these messages can instill an even more damaging set of core beliefs about the self that, when examined, qualify as traumatic. Trauma derives from the Greek work traumatikos meaning "wound." Professionals and diagnosticians continue to develop labels and technical rubrics for studying trauma and its clinical manifestations. Yet, from a humanitarian standpoint, we can simply define trauma as a wound—physical, emotional, verbal, sexual, or spiritual. And the wounds of the bisexual experiences are ones that I know all too well.

According to the adaptive information processing model developed by Dr. Francine Shapiro, the creator of eye movement desensitization and reprocessing (EMDR) therapy, we learn things about ourselves and the world around us as a result of adverse life experiences. We internalize the messages that come with these learnings. These messages can serve us or help us adapt; think messages like "I'm a survivor." Or these messages can create a belief structure that paralyzes us. Messages like "I am defective," "I am weak," or "I am permanently damaged," are examples of such culprits when we consider trauma in general. For many bisexuals and other marginalized individuals, the messages themselves may cause the wounding, further crystallizing those negative core beliefs in the limbic brain, the center of emotion and learning. Levis and Siniego coined the term oppressive cognitions, accurately naming this phenomenon. Let's further explore each of the messages introduced at the beginning of the book to discover how this dynamic of oppressive cognition plays out for bisexuals.

"There's no such thing as bisexuality." Many bisexual individuals hear this message from family, friends, and society at large. Sadly, even clinical professionals may declare this untruth as medical fact. Perhaps even more devastating is when bisexuals hear this message from other queer-identified individuals. This general message usually follows up with the opinion that coming out as bisexual is merely the first step in coming out as homosexual. The deeper message in all of this nonsense is that you don't exist. That, who you are, how you identify, everything that feels natural about your sexuality and/or sexual expression is invalid. I can think of few other messages that ring more oppressive. Many bisexuals, myself included, are proud of our identities. We delight in being able to form attractions to all genders, even if it's in various degrees and at different times in our lives. To further educate yourself on this more accurate definition of bisexuality, consider checking out the work of Dr. Fritz Klein, the first psychiatrist to fully validate our existence in his 1978 book, The Bisexual Option.

You're just confused and trying to sort things out. Our American society and many other global cultures tend to freak out over anything that isn't binary. Black or white, good or bad, fat or skinny, Coke or Pepsi, Democrat or Republican, gay or straight. If you can't neatly check one box, then there is something inherently wrong with you. Bisexuals are especially vulnerable to being attacked for not fitting the binary because our sexual identity, by its nature, shatters the very idea of binary. For people who can't conceptualize the notion of continuum, or variations in sexual attraction/expression, it's easy to slap the label of "confused" or even "attention seeking" on bisexuals. So much for shades of gray in a binary world.

The oppressive cognitions at play here: "I am defective," "There is something wrong with me," or any semantic variation on those statements. These messages can internalize in a uniquely damaging way because, for many of us, claiming the connection to our bisexuality is the most natural thing we could ever do. That natural connection, met with messages of "You're confused" can set off a tremendous amount of dissonance, distortion, and pain. Imagine if people explained the most vital aspect of your identity through the lens of confusion; that labeling is what bisexuals experience on a near daily basis.

"You'll have sex with anyone." Bisexuals are also used to hearing jabs that directly or indirectly imply that we're easy, naturally more promiscuous, or more willing to use our sexuality to get ahead. Most of us have had the old Woody Allen adage thrown in our direction, "Bisexuality immediately doubles your chances of a date on Saturday night." Consider how mainstream movies and TV usually portray bisexual characters or storylines. Think Frank Underwood from House of Cards or Analise Keating from How to Get Away with Murder. Typically, the bisexuality is featured as a component of their deceitfulness or as evidence of how broken they really are. You rarely see a healthy, whole, good-natured bisexual in mainstream entertainment. The traumatic messages at play here are obvious: "I am devious or deceitful." "I am broken because of who I am." Even the darkness of "Who I am will hurt other or put others in harm's way," can manifest internally when others communicate the stereotype that bisexuals are hypersexual and devious.

***

These three cognitions, while some of the most popular, are not exhaustive. Many of us, myself included struggle with beliefs like "I cannot fit in," or "There is no place for someone like me in this world." Within the LGBTQ+ community at large, bisexuals are often accused of having a level of privilege that insulates us from the rigors of living as an out person in a largely intolerant society. The fact that it may be easier for us to pass as straight or hide out in straight marriages is often cited to support this privilege. Debating what constitutes privilege extends the scope of this essay. I simply note my experience that a great deal of pain can come with this privilege. Oregon Governor Kate Brown, the first openly bisexual U.S. governor, described her experience in a way that resonates with me at my core—Sometimes I feel like I'm living with a foot in both worlds, never really belonging in either."

Navigating that dance is tricky, and it can leave us torn up inside. That was certainly the case for me.

I was especially vulnerable to hearing the messages I've highlighted in this piece from people who did not realize that I identified as bisexual, particularly when I was married to a cisgender man. Part of my healing requires me to deal with the wounds that I've acquired as a result of internalizing many of these oppressive cognitions throughout my life. In comparison to other traumas I've had to address that are not specific to sexuality, I can attest that this healing around the trauma of the bisexual experience has proven some of the most difficult I've had to embrace. My marriage to that cisgender man did not survive me coming out fully and unapologetically in all areas of my life, even though he knew that I was bisexual when we got married. There is something about coming out with abandon that demanded me to live a life of radical authenticity and what can I say ... just about every man with whom I've been romantically involved cannot seem to handle that.

In my own recovery, I've drawn tremendous strength from the wisdom of Cuban-French writer, poet, and champion of the erotic feminine, Anaïs Nin. One of her most famous quotes, which appeared in her journals, proclaims: "Shame is the lie someone told you about yourself." When I consider the messages hurled at me from all directions, I can now see them as lies. I've required a great deal of support, validation from understanding figures, and my own psychotherapy to arrive at this place. If you are an ally to bisexual individuals, consider the role that you can play in helping bisexual individuals begin to realize a new truth about themselves. If you are a bisexually identified, sexually fluid, or a questioning individual, my hope for you is that you can find the support and help you need to give these messages, these lies that have wounded you, the big middle finger.

May you find your new truth.

This essay adapted and edited from an article of the same title by the author that first appeared on the blog "Psyched" (2016).

Jamie Marich, Ph.D., LPCC-S, LICDC-CS, REAT, RYT-500, RMT. Dr. Jamie Marich describes herself as a facilitator of transformative experiences. A clinical trauma specialist, expressive artist, writer, yogini, performer, short filmmaker, Reiki master, TEDx speaker, and recovery advocate, she unites all of these elements in her mission to inspire healing in others. She began her career as a humanitarian aid worker in Bosnia-Herzegovina from 2000-2003, primarily teaching English and music. Jamie travels internationally teaching on topics related to trauma, EMDR therapy, expressive arts, mindfulness, and yoga, while maintaining a private practice and online education operations in her home base of Warren, OH.

Marich is the founder of the Institute for Creative Mindfulness and the developer of the *Dancing Mindfulness* approach to expressive arts therapy. She is also the co-creator of the *Yoga Unchained* approach to trauma-informed yoga, and the developer of Yoga for Clinicians. Marich is the author of *EMDR Made Simple: 4 Approaches for Using EMDR with Every Client* (2011), *Trauma and the Twelve Steps: A Complete Guide for Recovery En-*

hancement (2012), *Creative Mindfulness* (2013), *Trauma Made Simple: Competencies in Assessment, Treatment, and Working with Survivors, and Dancing Mindfulness: A Creative Path to Healing and Transformation* (2015). Marich co-authored *EMDR Therapy & Mindfulness for Trauma-Focused Care* along with her colleague, Dr. Stephen Dansiger, which was released by Springer Publishing in 2017. *Process Not Perfection: Expressive Arts Solutions for Trauma Recovery* was released in April 2019. North Atlantic Books published a revised and expanded edition of *Trauma and the 12 Steps* in the Summer of 2020.

Marich's own company, Creative Mindfulness Media, produced a daily meditation reader and workbook to accompany the *Trauma and the 12 Steps* project in the Autumn of 2020, in collaboration with Dr. Stephen Danisger. *The New York Times* featured Marich's writing and work on *Dancing Mindfulness* in 2017 and 2020. NALGAP: The Association of Gay, Lesbian, Bisexual, Transgender Addiction Professionals and Their Allies awarded Jamie with their esteemed President's Award in 2015 for her work as an LGBT advocate. The EMDR International Association (EMDRIA) granted Jamie the 2019 Advocacy in EMDR Award for use of her public platform in media and in the addiction field to advance awareness about EMDR therapy and reduce stigma around mental health. Marich also sits on the clinical workgroup of EMDRIA's prestigious Council of Scholars.

Tips for Getting to the Other Side

Not knowing how to tell the people in your life about your sexuality often stops people from sharing their truth for years or even a lifetime. The following is a list of real conversation prompts used by the womxn in the "Bite Out of Life" Facebook group as they bravely came out to family members. We hope this helps you navigate these difficult and often surprisingly welcomed conversations.

**Some of the ways you may start to open up to your
PARTNER about your sexuality:**
"I need to have an honest conversation with you about my sexual needs and desires."

"I need to start this by telling you I love you and ... I am gay."

"I have been thinking a lot lately, and I realize that I have a deep knowing that I want to explore sex with other women."

"There is a woman at work who is flirting with me, and I am ... intrigued."

"I feel like something inside of me has awakened."

"I wrote down some thoughts and want to sit with you as you read them."

"Before I met you, I was in love with someone. That someone was a woman."

"Well, the problem is, you have a dick."

Tips: Be honest. Keep other issues and problems separate from this conversation. If this is your first conversation, his initial reaction may not be his lasting one. Do seek the help of a therapist.

Some of the ways you may start to open up to your KIDS about your sexuality:

"I believe that love is love, and people should be able to choose who they love and live with."

"If I were to marry again, I believe it will be to a woman."

"I need to tell you something about me personally."

"There is a part of the story about Dad and I divorcing that we haven't told you yet. I'm gay."

"You are so open with your friends about sexuality. I am proud of you."

"When I was young, the world was a very different place, and it felt very unaccepting for people who were different. That made me sad and scared because I thought there might have been something about me that was different. I still do, but it feels much safer now, and I feel very loved and accepted, so I want to tell you that I identify as ..."

Tips: Talk to your kids when they have time and space to process, like over a long weekend or holiday. Kids understand love and can sense deception. Knowing the truth may be a relief to them. Although it is true that some people judge LG-

BTQ+ people, studies have shown that a parent's self-respect, honesty, and pride speak louder than homophobia.

One last note...

"Not disclosing sexual orientation, it turns out, leads to chronic stress and a buildup of the stress hormone cortisol, which results in wear and tear on multiple biological systems," reports Dr. Rick Nauert of the Rocky Mountain University of Health Professions. "Lesbians, gays, and bisexuals who have 'come out' have lower stress hormone levels and fewer symptoms of anxiety, depression, and burnout."

Acknowledgements

I would like to thank my clients, podcast listeners, and the womxn in the Bite Out of Life community for trusting me to hold space for your exploration of sexuality and pleasure.

I especially thank the liberated womxn who bravely shared their stories in this book.

I want to thank my life and business coaches Megan Jo Wilson, Shannon Rose, and Kevin Palmieri for mirroring my audaciousness back to me every time I forgot who I was.

I wish to thank the publishing team of GWN Publishing - Lil and Cindy for believing in me and taking me on as a passion project. Kate and Linda for editing this work.

Thank you to my amazing friends and family who not only accept me for all of my truths, quirks, and crazy ideas, but actually celebrate me when I push the edge.

While I'm at it, thank you to Brene Brown, Glennon Doyle, Elizabeth Gilbert, and Tig Notaro for cracking me up and cracking me open with your wisdom and stories...I have crushes on you all and hope we meet someday.

And even though he was not thrilled I was writing this book, I want to honor and thank my husband, John, for being understanding, supportive, and willing to stay with me on this bumpy ride called marriage.

Finally, I wish to acknowledge my children, who have each said in their own unique way upon hearing about this book "Go, Mom. You do you." It took 50 years to build the courage to talk about my truths, and in seconds, the three of you opened your hearts and made it all seem perfectly aligned and freeing. I love you all.

About the Author

Pasha Marlowe holds a masters in Marriage and Family Therapy and works as a laughter and pleasure coach. She is the host of the Let Pleasure be the Measure Podcast and the leader of the Midlife Mischief and Merriment fb group. She coaches womxn individually and in groups and empowers them to speak their radical truths, claim their desires, and then release them into the universe via a conversation, book, speech, or comedy routine. Her eight-week coaching program ROAR with LAUGHTER culminates in a live comedy performance. Pasha believes that holding our stories, shame, and secrets in our bodies leads to chronic illness and pain. Her greatest pleasure is hanging out with her three children and exploring new adventures and ideas.

CONTACT INFO:
Email: pasha@pashamarlowe.com
Website: pashamarlowe.com
FB: https://www.facebook.com/Pashamarlowecoaching
IG: @pashamarlowe
Podcast: Let Pleasure be the Measure:
https://podcasts.apple.com/us/podcast/
let-pleasure-be-the-measure/id1548282200

www.ingramcontent.com/pod-product-compliance
Lightning Source LLC
Chambersburg PA
CBHW050745030426
42336CB00012B/1658